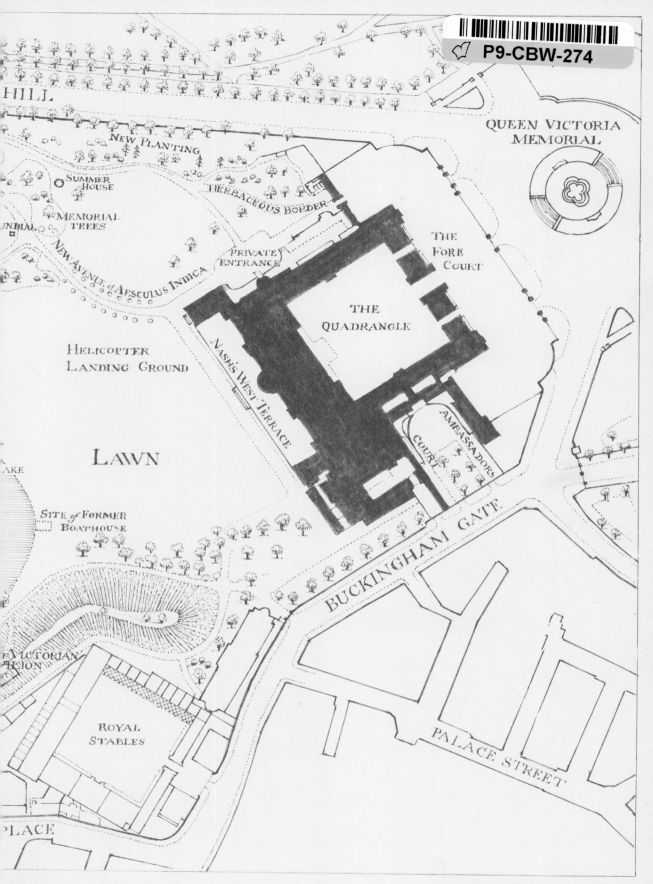

Endpaper drawing by Hugh Robson

Other books by Peter Coats

A Book of Gardens
Roses
Great Gardens of the Western World
House & Garden Garden Book
Great Gardens of Britain
Flowers in History
Garden Decoration
Plants for Connoisseurs
Of Generals & Gardens—An Autobiography

The Gardens of Buckingham Palace

Peter Coats

MICHAEL JOSEPH
London

First published in Great Britain by
Michael Joseph Ltd
52 Bedford Square
London WC1B 3EF
1978

ISBN 0 7181 1607 0

Filmset and printed by
BAS Printers Limited, Over Wallop, Hampshire

Contents

Foreword by H.R.H. Prince Philip, The Duke of Edinburgh

Introduction

Part I History

I	The Mulberry Gardens	14
II	Henry VIII and the Early Days of St James's	19
III	Goring House	21
IV	The Extravagant Earl of Arlington	25
V	The Duke of Buckingham	30
VI	'Princess Buckingham'	38
VII	Buckingham House becomes the Queen's House	42
VIII	Queen Charlotte	47
IX	The Garden is Landscaped	52
X	George IV and William IV	58
XI	Queen Victoria	61
XII	The Garden Pavilion	65
XIII	Garden Parties	70

Part II The Garden Today

XIV	The Terrace and Lawn	78
XV	The Lake	87
XVI	The Trees	91
XVII	Camellias, Magnolias and other Shrubs	99
XVIII	The Herbaceous Border	108
XIX	The Rose Garden	114
XX	The Grey Border	117

XXI	The Cascade	121
XXII	Garden Ornaments	123
	(a) The Waterloo Vase, the Admiralty	123
	Temple Summer House and the Sundial	
	(b) The Flamingoes	130

Part III Wild Life

XXIII	The Survey	134
XXIV	Wild Plants	137
XXV	Birds	140
XXVI	Fish and Amphibians	143
XXVII	Lepidoptera	148
XXVIII	Spiders and Insects	154
	Postscript	156
	Index	158

Acknowledgements

The quoted passages from the Royal Archives are included by gracious permission of Her Majesty the Queen. I should like to thank Her Majesty Queen Elizabeth the Queen Mother for kindly letting me show her photograph on page 125, and H.R.H. The Duke of Edinburgh for writing the Foreword.

I have expressed my gratitude in the text to the British Entomological and Natural History Society for permission to quote so extensively from their publication of December 1964, to Mr. Fred Nutbeam and to Mr. David McClintock, and I would like to add very special thanks to Dr. J. D. Bradley of the Commonwealth Institute of Entomology for his great help and interest throughout. Thanks, too, are due to Mr. Barry Gibbs whose first idea it was that a book about the Royal garden should be written, to Mr. Bill Travers and to Miss Virginia McKenna, who recently made a film, 'The Queen's Garden'; to Mrs. David Verey, and to many other helpful friends. Not least, the police in the Palace Gardens. I am grateful, too, to Miss Winifred Marshall, and to Miss Joanne Levin, for typing the manuscript.

List of Colour Plates

facing page

Mulberry leaves with silk worms   16
Strelitzia reginae   17
Queen Charlotte (1744–1818)   17
A side room of the Garden Pavilion   32
A contorted Sweet Chestnut   33
Drifts of crocus and an Indian Chestnut   48
Daffodils and the new Indian Chestnut
avenue   49
The Waterloo Vase   64
Camellias in early spring   64
Magnolia soulangeana   65
Magnolia soulangeana 'Picture'   65
Spring blossom   80
Pieris forrestii   80
Early summer tulips   81
Rhododendrons   96
The cascade   96
The Admiralty Temple Summer House   97

between pages 120–21

The Palace from the north-west
Delphiniums and 'Princess Alexandra'
geraniums
Golden tones of the late summer border
The Grey Border
Geraniums growing in the greenhouse area
A garden party flower arrangement
Flamingoes on the lake

facing page

Japanese bronze cranes   128
The lake in late summer   129
A collection of butterflies and moths   144
Moths caught in the Royal Garden   145

BUCKINGHAM PALACE.

What happens on the other side of a wall is always an intriguing question and when the wall is in the middle of London and encloses the garden of Buckingham Palace it is positively tantalising. All is now revealed in this history and detailed anatomy of this piece of land and all its plant and animal residents and visitors.

The author has not just researched every aspect most carefully and thoroughly, he has succeeded in converting the results into an interesting and most readable book.

It is of course rather an unusual garden anyway in that it is used for all sorts of activities unknown to most public and private gardens. For one thing I suspect it has the distinction of being the oldest helicopter landing site in continuous use in central London. First used just before the Coronation in 1953 hardly a week goes by without at least one arrival and departure. It is comforting to know that this does not seem to have had any noticeable effect on its animal population.

1977.

Introduction

This seems to be the first book ever to be written about the garden of Buckingham Palace. There have been many books about the Palace, its history and its contents, but none exclusively about the garden. In *Royal Gardens*, by Cyril Ward published in 1912, there were chapters devoted to the gardens at Windsor Castle, at Balmoral and Sandringham but none about the garden of Buckingham Palace. In a recent best-selling book on the British Monarchy, the Palace garden is only mentioned once in the preface to say that it is big, which it is, and twice in the text, to say that H.M. The Queen, as a little girl, had once fallen into the lake, and that she has used the Summer House, where King George VI used to work, as a Girl Guide Headquarters.

To most Londoners, and visitors to London, the garden of Buckingham Palace appears to be a vast, leafy, unknown space enclosed on three sides by Constitution Hill, Grosvenor Place and Buckingham Palace Road. And yet it is a garden which is seen by many thousands of people every year. By more, probably, than many private gardens that are open regularly to the public.

H.M. The Queen and H.R.H. The Duke of Edinburgh give, on an average, three, sometimes four, garden parties a year. Nine thousand guests are invited to each. Twenty-seven, or possibly thirty-six, thousand people is not a bad start. And the garden is used for other public purposes. For Not Forgotten Association parties, Presentation of Colours and the like – which would add several more thousand to the total. It would be wrong to say that the garden is not as fully used as it might be.

As author, I should like to express my gratitude to H.M. The Queen and H.R.H. The Duke of Edinburgh for sanctioning the writing of the story of the garden at Buckingham Palace, and for allowing me constant access to the garden for photography

and study of the plants and of the wild life, in which the garden abounds, and which adds greatly to its interest.

My thanks are due, too, to the Head Gardener at the Palace, Mr. Fred Nutbeam, who has been a most agreeable and informative companion, in spite of bad health, and many calls on his time. All the members of the not-very-large garden staff have been most helpful.

I must say a special word about the wild life section of this book.

Though I pride myself on being something of a practical gardener, knowledgeable about plants and trees, and a keen garden historian, I admit to being an amateurish ornithologist, and almost totally ignorant as a lepidopterist.

Until I started to describe the wild life of the Royal garden I am ashamed to admit that I did not even know the meaning of the word hymenoptera. My experience, in my garden life up to date, of wild life, had entirely been gained through strenuous efforts to eradicate it. For years, I have waged war on aphids, black spiders, slugs, saw-flies and mealy bug. I have mercilessly shot rabbits (or wired them out), poisoned rats, and set traps for moles. I plead not guilty to shooting many birds, though at times I have been highly tried by predatory bullfinches and pigeons. I admit to having once shot at a heron which had eaten five out of my six goldfish (all personal friends, and named after famous film stars). But being a bad shot, I only detached a few tail feathers.

Therefore, for the material of the third section of this book, I would like to admit a great debt to Mr. David McClintock, and to a learned publication of which he was the chief instigator and contributor, entitled *Natural History of the Garden of Buckingham Palace*, published in the Proceedings and Transactions of the South London (now British) Entomological and Natural History Society for 1963, and devoted to the history, in the widest sense, of the garden of Buckingham Palace. This book – small in size, but full of meat, 'Infinite riches in a little room' – has been the source of virtually all my information about the remarkable variety of wild life to be found in the Royal garden. It is still available and makes fascinating reading.

If one took some liberties with Lewis Carroll, and then quoted the Walrus's list of talking-points, backwards in true

Looking Glass fashion, one would have four apposite lines with which to end this Introduction.

> The time has come the Author said
> To talk of many things.
> Of birds, and moths, and butterflies
> Of cabbages – and Kings.

Peter Coats
Al Albany
Summer 1977

(*overleaf*) The garden façade, showing Nash's unpopular dome and the roof-line before it was raised to include another storey. From the Crace collection.

Part I
History

The Mulberry Gardens

The story of the garden at Buckingham Palace may fairly be said to start three hundred and fifty years ago, in the reign of King James I. Early in his reign, the King, envious of the thriving silk manufactures of France at Lyons and Tours, decided to sponsor silk-making in England. To this end, mulberry trees, of which the leaves form the silkworms' staple and favourite diet, were to be imported from all over Europe, and planted in some waste land to the west of St James's Park.

King James I 1603–25 endeavoured to establish the silk industry in England and had mulberry trees, to provide food for silk worms, planted in part of St James's Park. This was the first garden near the present site of Buckingham Palace.

The King was enthusiastic about the scheme. He envisaged mulberry groves, not only in London but all over the country, and a Royal letter went forth, signed by the Royal hand, to all the Lords Lieutenants.

King James is said to have planted the Black Mulberry. Silk worms prefer the leaves of the White Mulberry.

It is a principall part of that Christian care which appertaineth to sovereigntie, to endeavour, by all meanes possible . . . to increase, among their people, the knowledge and practise of all artes and trades . . . thus raysing and encreasing them in wealth and abundance. . . . And, therefore, we have thought good hereby to let you understand, that although, in suffering this invention to take place, we doe shew our selves somewhat an adversarie to our profit, which, in the matter of our customes for silke brought from beyond the seas, will receive diminution: neverthelesse, when there is question of so great and publique utilitie, and whereby . . . we are content that our private benefit shall give way to our publique . . .

. . . if you, and other your neighbours, will be content to take some good quantities here [of mulberry trees], to distribute upon your own lands: we are content to acknowledge . . . are things so naturally pleasing to our owne disposition, as we shall take it for an argument of extraordinairie affectation towards our person; . . . and shall esteeme that, in furthering the same, they seeke to further our honour and contentment, who having seene in few yeares space past, that our brother, the French King, hath, since his coming to that Crowne, both begunne and brought to perfection the making of silkes in his country . . . whereby he hath wonne to himself honour, and to his subjectes a mervailous increase of wealth, would account it no little happinesse to us, if the same worke . . . might, in our time, produce the fruits which there it hath done.

Thus King James expressed himself prepared to sacrifice some of his own revenue derived from the duties levied on French silk for the good of his English subjects. 'The dream of an idealist?' asks Bruce Graeme. * 'Perhaps, but who can deny that there was a firm foundation for his vision of a future great

*The story of Buckingham Palace by Bruce Graeme: Hutchinson 1928

An old print from *The Universal Magazine* showing how mulberry leaves were stored for feeding silk worms.

OPPOSITE
Mulberry leaves with silk worms, *Bombyx mori* and two Tiger Moths, *Arctia caja,* with larva.

industry? Silk had already established the wealth of past and forgotten cities and empires: Babylon, Damascus, Tyre . . . all fostered a silk industry.'

For a time King James's enthusiasm never faltered. On the 5th January 1607 a licence was given to one William Stallenge to publish a book of *Instructions for the planting and increase of Mulberry Trees, breeding of Silkworms and the making of Silk.*

Thus landowners throughout the country were urged to 'purchase, and plant, 10,000 mulberry trees, to be delivered to purchasers in March or April next, at the rate of 6/- a thousand', and the book of instructions was promised shortly. Stallenge was the moving spirit of the enterprise, and was, in the final event, the only participant who made anything out of it. At the end of 1609 he was paid £935 for 'the charge of four acres taken in for His Majesty's use, near to his Palace of

To the Right Honourable. *Countefs of Ailesford*
This Plate is most humbly Dedicated by her Ladyships most obliged & obedient Serv.ᵗ
Moses Harris

APERTO VIVERE VOTO

Westminster, for the planting of mulberry trees, together with the charge of walling, levelling and planting thereof, subscribed by the surveyors of His Majesty's Works, and the said William Stallenge'.

The area was duly enclosed and planted, and soon became known as the Mulberry Gardens. The precious worms themselves (the larvae of *Bombyx mori*) were introduced; – but it seems that the trees were slow in producing enough leaves for them to feed on, for two years later, in 1611, Stallenge was buying-in mulberry leaves 'and other necessaries'. More expenditure followed, and for no return. In spite of Royal enthusiasm (King James even took some silkworms with him on his 'progresses') the infant silk industry promised to be a failure – and for one very good reason. The mulberry trees King James ordered by the thousand, some of which may still be growing in England today, were *Morus nigra* – the black mulberry – a native tree of many of the cooler Oriental countries. The black mulberry bears excellent fruit – hence its popularity; and silkworms can, with difficulty, be induced to feed on its rough glossy leaves. But they infinitely prefer to dine off the lighter green, silkier leaves of a different and more delicate mulberry – *Morus alba* – the white mulberry, native of

OPPOSITE

(*inset*) When *Strelitzia reginae* was named after Queen Charlotte (born a Princess of Mecklenburg Stelitz) the botanist Sir Joseph Banks described it as a just tribute to her botanical zeal and knowledge. Drawing by Sydenham Edwards in *The New Botanic Garden*, 1812.

Queen Charlotte (1744–1818) in front of Buckingham House, which became her property by Act of Parliament in 1775, and henceforth was known as the Queen's House (*see chapters VII and VIII*). From a print in the Crace collection.

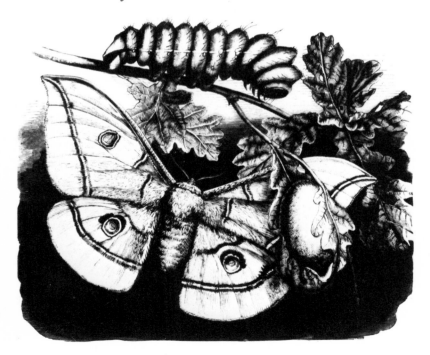

Attempts were once made to induce silk worms to feed on oak leaves.

southern Europe. The white mulberry is not really happy in a northern climate, hence the ultimate failure of James I's grandiose scheme for introducing the silkworm industry into England.

Recently another theory has been suggested – that King James and his advisers could not have been so badly informed as to have planted the wrong sort of mulberry, and that the silkworm scheme must have failed for other reasons – probably climatic, or the use of wrong methods of culture.

Whatever the true story, the Mulberry Gardens continued in existence for another forty odd years. In 1628 Charles I entrusted Lord Aston, a Staffordshire landowner, with the 'keeping of His Majesty's Mulberry Gardens at St James and of the silk worms and houses thereunto appertaining, with the yearly fee of £60 during his life and that of his son and heir apparant, on surrender of Jasper Stallenge'. Presumably Jasper was the son or grandson of William Stallenge, the chief instigator of the scheme.

Lord Aston was no more successful than his predecessor; and from now on, the history of the Mulberry Gardens becomes obscure. Bruce Graeme complains that in spite of patient research 'in the dusty volumes of the British Museum, in the ageing manuscripts of the Harleian Miscellany . . . in the Issues of the Exchequer or in the Domestic series of State Papers . . .', it is impossible to discover more of the history of the Mulberry Gardens; but the fact of their having once existed is of interest even if the story of their gradual decline from their original purpose is less so.

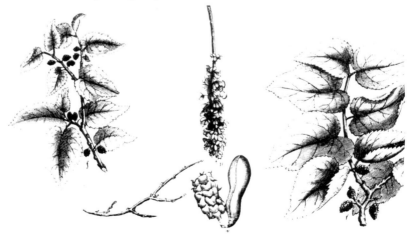

Henry VIII and the Early Days of St James's

The Mulberry Gardens fade from our story for a quarter of a century until the famous diarist and gardener, John Evelyn, mentions them during Cromwell's Commonwealth. But before carrying the story of the Mulberry Gardens one stage further, there is some point in looking at the countryside in which they were set.

King Henry VIII was the first English monarch to lay a royal hand on the marshy, low-lying wasteland to the west of the palaces of Westminster and Whitehall. While married to Anne Boleyn, he seized an ancient hospital which had been founded in the 12th century and which was, at the time of their ejection, the crumbling asylum of fourteen leper maidens. The hospital lay a quarter of a mile west of the village of Charing; it was demolished, and on its site the enamoured King Henry built a hunting lodge for himself and Anne. The hospital had been dedicated to St James the Less, and the name of St James was given, not only to King Henry's new building but, in time, to the whole area round about. The walls of the hunting lodge were decorated with carved lovers' knots and entwined H's and A's (one still is to be seen in the St James's Palace Presence Chamber), and Henry and Anne rode out happily from their new love box, to hunt in the nearby countryside, then quite wild. In due course, the marshy land to the south and west was drained, enclosed, and taken for the King's own. In time it was to form the nucleus of what is now the Royal Park of St James, and it was on the edge of this enclosure that King James gave the piece of ground for his famous mulberries.

What grew there before the mulberries were planted?

In William Camden's survey, *Britannia, or a Chorographical Description of Great Britain and Ireland*, which was written in Latin in the 16th century and translated in the early 18th century by Edmond Gibson, afterwards Bishop of Lincoln, a list is given of some of the plants then growing wild in

Middlesex. Today, some would be considered, if not rarities, certainly plants which one would be surprised to find growing wild in hedgerows or by the sides of streams almost anywhere in the country. A few of these include *Argemone laciniata*, described as a 'Bastard Poppey', an annual plant now only found in specialists' gardens; the rare moss, *Muscus palustris*, a 'small upright bog-moss' which in those days could be found in marshy ground at Hounslow and near Westminster: *Xyris foetida*, the 'Stinking Gladdon', an iris which you would have to travel a long way from London today to find growing wild; and *Chamaemelum nobilis*, which is described as having been found thriving in 'Tuttle-Fields' [Tothill Fields], Westminster', and is particularly interesting in view of the chamomile which is today incorporated in the lawn of the garden at Buckingham Palace. Another plant which four hundred years ago appeared to flourish by the side of ditches and streams in the London area, according to Camden, was *Osmunda regalis*, the Royal fern. Osmunda today is only to be found naturalized in the gardens of connoisseurs, and there are several imposing clumps growing by the water's edge of the lake in the Palace garden, but they were certainly specially planted.

Osmunda achieved its Royal connotation from the legend that Osmund, an early King of Britain, hid his daughter in a clump of fern to conceal her from the attentions of the invading and amorous Danes.

Goring House

Returning to the 17th century, and the story of the Mulberry Garden: Lord Aston's son had sold his interest in the gardens to Lord Goring in 1640, and it was the luxurious and pleasure-loving Goring who was to build the first great house in the area to the south of the Mulberry Gardens themselves. Goring House, the progenitor of all the subsequent houses on the site, was an imposing brick house with two projecting wings and a mansard roof surmounted by a vast cupola. Unlike the future houses on the site, it faced south towards what now is Buckingham Palace Road.

It was to enlarge the ground of his new house that Lord Goring, just before the outbreak of the Civil War, bought the Mulberry Garden area and 'all that watercourse in or near the highway . . . and the soil of the same, with liberty to build on the said watercourse and highway . . .' The watercourse was the Tyburn, one of London's two lost rivers which now runs entirely underground, though its waters feed the lake in St James's Park; as the waters of another lost river, the

Goring House was the first large house to be built on the site. It was bought by Lord Arlington in 1675, and became famous for its 'wantoness and profusion'. It burned down, was rebuilt and renamed Arlington House.

Westbourne, feed the Serpentine. And Lord Goring further added to his property by buying two large fields, Upper Crow and Lower Crow, which now make up most of the site of Buckingham Palace Garden, Upper Crow stretching as far as the present Hyde Park Corner.

Lord Goring liked spending money, but in spite of his large fortune, he was frequently in financial difficulties. Following the enlargement of his property there were frequent legal tangles, and the Civil War which broke out in 1642 and resulted in his exile, added to the complications. Suffice it to say that when Lord Goring, by now Earl of Norwich, returned from exile, the property had passed through so many hands that he had difficulty in proving his title to it. He invoked the aid of his cousin, Henry Bennet, later Earl of Arlington, who was in actual occupation of the house, to speak to the King on his behalf, but to no avail. And in 1672, twelve years after the Restoration, Lord Norwich lost his estate, and the Mulberry Gardens passed officially into the possession of Lord Arlington; three years later, Goring House did as well.

'With Arlington's occupation of the house,' writes Clifford Smith* with something of a sigh of relief, 'we reach the end of the tedious phase of the property's history in which litigation seems to have been endless. In place of lawsuits and rapid changes of tenancy we can deal with the home of a cultivated gentleman who surrounded himself with the choicest art and society. The invaluable diarists of the epoch from time to time let fall illuminating comments on his mansion.'

Meanwhile, at the Restoration, the Mulberry Gardens had come into their own as a place of resort. Six years before, John Evelyn had visited them and had been entertained there by his friend Lady Gerrard: he described them as 'the only place of refreshment in town for people of the best quality to be cheated at; Cromwell and his partisans having shut up and seized on Spring Gardens, which till now had been the usual rendezvous for the ladies and gallants at this season'.

With the return of the King and a frivolous Court to London, the Mulberry Gardens were no longer a breeding ground for silkworms – that enterprise had all but been abandoned – but a breeding ground for scandal and illicit exchanges. The gardens had become a pleasure resort for Londoners, only to be rivalled in later years by Ranelagh and Vauxhall.

Buckingham Palace by H. Clifford Smith: *Country Life* 1931

The houses 'wherein the royal silkworms had once lived their lives of ease and luxury' were converted into wine-booths and eating shops. Among the leafy groves of mulberry trees were built green arbours which soon became popular places of assignation.

Sir Charles Sedley (whose illegitimate grand-daughter was to become, by a curious chance, the owner of the future Buckingham Palace) named one of his plays *The Mulberry Garden* and made it clear that the garden had become one of the sights of London: Ned Estridge says: 'These country ladies, for the first month, take up their places in the Mulberry Garden, as early as a citizen's wife at a new play', and the sophisticated Modish replies, 'and for the most part are as easily discovered, they have always something on that is just left off by the better

Samuel Pepys (1633–1703) found the Mulberry Gardens frequented by 'a rascally, whoring, roguing sort of people'. Sketch by Hugh Robson.

sort,' to which Estridge adds, 'They are the Antipodes of the court, for, when a fashion sets there, it rises among them.'

And in another scene of the play the unsophisticated Olivia Everyoung expresses her delight in a visit to the Mulberry Gardens, in a long speech: ' 'Tis much better than a long walk at home, for in my opinion, half a score of young men and fine ladies, well drest, are a greater ornament to a garden than a wilderness of sycamores, orange and lemon trees; and the rustling of silk petticoats better music than the purling of streams, chirping of birds, or any of our country entertainments.'

And in a play of Etherege, *She Wou'd if she Cou'd*, two young nieces of Sir Joslin Jolly, Ariana and Gatty, returning home after a flirtatious romp in the Gardens, are reprimanded by the shocked Lady Cockwood, with the words 'without the company of a relation! or some discreet body to justify your reputations?'

But the Gardens were not noted as a resort for 'discreet bodies' – in fact very much the opposite. Even Pepys – who was not exactly prudish – found them a 'silly place . . . and but little company, and . . . a rascally, whoring roguing sort of people, only a wilderness, that is somewhat pretty, but rude . . .'

William Wycherly in his play *The Humourists* makes one of his characters, Friske, ask '. . . why does not Your Ladyship frequent the Mulberry Gardens oftener?' and another character adds '. . . it was very full, Madame, of ladies and gentlemen who made love together till twelve o'clock at night'.

The poet Dryden (1631–1700) was one of the more innocent visitors to the Gardens and is on record as going there to eat mulberry tarts. But by the middle of the 1670s the popularity of the Gardens had declined, and soon after the final acquisition of the whole property by Lord Arlington, they were closed.

The Extravagant Earl of Arlington

Henry Bennet, Earl of Arlington, was a life-long favourite of Charles II, and one of the less scrupulous members of the unscrupulous Cabal. He was wounded at the engagement at Andover in the Civil War, which left a permanent scar on his nose over which he invariably wore a foppish crescent of black

Henry Bennet, Earl of Arlington (1618–1685) wearing the half-moon-shaped plaster on his nose as a reminder of a wound received in the Civil War while fighting for the King. A member of the Cabal, he planted a garden at Arlington House where, according to Dryden, 'The painted tulip and the blushing rose
A blooming wilderness of sweets compose'
From a portrait by Sir Peter Lely.

plaster, which is clearly visible in his portrait; this affectation was frequently made fun of, perhaps unfairly, by his political opponents.

During his ownership, Goring House became a famous centre for entertaining. Arlington spent thousands on beautifying the house and its surroundings, aided and abetted by his wife who, while 'good natured and obliging' was 'incalculably extravagant, fond of luxurious living and sumptuous surroundings'. John Evelyn – who likened the outside of Goring House to an ill-built villa – praised, though grudgingly, the interior as being filled with 'so rich furniture as I had seldom seen: to this excess of superfluity are we now arrived . . . even to wantoness and profusion'.

Arlington's political career had its ups and downs, and in 1674 he was impeached by the House of Commons. The impeachment failed, but Arlington thought it best to resign his many offices, and retire to Bath. While he and his wife were there, they heard that Goring House, with all its treasures, 'its wantoness and profusion', had been burned to the ground.

Lord Arlington, with his passion for grandeur, lost no time in rebuilding. The new house, re-named Arlington House, was infinitely more splendid than its predecessor. Dryden was so impressed that he broke into verse; and composed a poem that

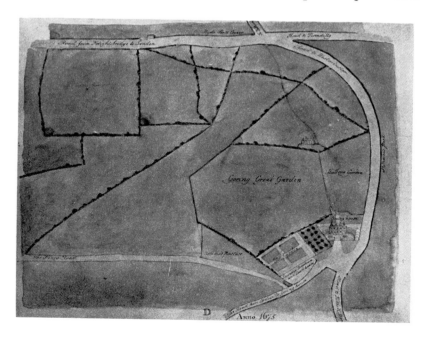

A plan of 1675 showing the position of the 'Goring Great Garden', the Mulberry Garden and Goring House. The house faced south. From the Crace collection.

26

is far too long to quote in full, but which contains some lines so redolent of the Baroque language of the time that it would be a pity not to include them, especially as some of them are the first mention – in literature, and in three centuries of English literature there are very few – of the gardens of what was one day to be Buckingham Palace.

First – the new house itself:

> Near those fair lawns, and intermingled groves
> Where gentle Zephyrs breathe, and sporting Loves;
> A frame there stands, that rears its beautious height
> And strikes with pleasing ravishment the sight . . .

Then – the surroundings, three hundred years ago:

> . . . opening buds their tender leaves display
> While the fair vales afford a smiling view
> And the fields glitter with the morning dew.
> No rattling wheel disturbes the peaceful ground
> Or wounds the ear with any jarring sound

Next, the garden:

> The beautious gardens charm the ravish'd sight,
> And surfeit every sense with soft delight;
> Where-e're we turn our still transported eyes,
> New scenes of Art, with Nature join'd, arise;
> We dwell indulgent on the lovely scene,
> The lengthen'd vista or the carpet green;
> A thousand graces bless th'enchanted ground,
> And throw promiscuous beauties all around.
> Within they fair parterres appear to view
> A thousand flowers of various form and hue
> There spotless lilies rear their sickly heads,
> And purple violets creep along the beds;
> Here shews the bright jonquil its gilded face,
> Join'd with the pale carnation's fairer grace;
> The painted tulip and the blushing rose
> A blooming wilderness of sweets compose.

There was also, it seems, a greenhouse . . .

Here a new wonder stops the wandering sight,
A dome whose walls and roof transmit the light;
Here foreign plants and trees exotic thrive,
And in the cold unfriendly climate live;
For when bleak winter chills the rolling year,
The guarded strangers find their safety here;
And Fenc'd from storms and inclement air,
They sweetly flourish ever green and fair;
Their lively buds they shoot, and blossoms show,
And gaily bloom amidst surrounding snow.

. . . and a terrace . . .

A curious terrace stops the wandering eye,
Where lovely jasmines fragrant shade supply:
Whose tender branches, in their pride array'd,
Invite the wanderer to the grateful shade;
From hence afar a various prospect lies;
Where artless Nature courts the ravished eyes.
The sight at once a thousand charms surveys,
And, pleas'd, o'er villages and forests strays;
Here harvests grow, and lawns appear, and woods,
And gently rising hills, – and distant floods.

And a special delight for lovers, who either

. . . spend the flying hours in amorous joy
Or through the maze forgetfully they stray
Lost in the pleasing sweetly winding way . . .

According to Dryden, Lord Arlington's garden must have
been a place of enchantment indeed.

Lady Isabella Bennet, the Arlingtons' only and adored child,
was married at the age of five to the King's natural son, the
Duke of Grafton. Though rough and uncouth, the Duke was
the best of Charles I's bastards, and he was to find a hero's
death at the Siege of Cork in 1690.

Arlington's life was spent in embellishing and enriching his
property of Arlington House and its gardens, of which his

beloved daughter was sole heiress. He died in 1685.

After the death of the Duke of Grafton the Duchess, having borne her valiant husband an only son, rented her house to the Devonshire family, and a contemporary survey of the Cities of London & Westminster describes Arlington House 'at the upper end of the Park westward' as 'a most neat box, sweetly sealed among gardens, besides the prospect of the park, and the adjoining fields'. And in another survey of the area of about the same date there is a fuller description:

> Arlington House, now being in the hands of my Lord of Devonshire, is a fair place, with good walls, both airy and shady. There are six of the greatest earthen pots that are anywhere else, being at least ten feet over within the edge, but they stand abroad, and have nothing in them but the holy-oak, an indifferent plant, which grows well enough in the ground. Their greenhouse is very well, and their green-yard excels, but their greens are not so bright and clean as farther off in the country, as if they suffered something from the smutty air of the town.

This proves two points: first, that the Devonshires were not imaginative gardeners, ilexes not being suitable plants for pots, however large, and second, that London was spreading towards Arlington House, through Pimlico, and out from Westminster to the north along Piccadilly, bringing grimy clouds of smoke from a thousand sea-coal fires with it.

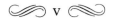

The Duke
of Buckingham

During the tenancy of the Duke of Devonshire there was yet another fire, and the house once more was badly damaged. In 1703, the year after Queen Anne's accession, the Duchess of Grafton sold the property to John Sheffield, Earl of Mulgrave, who demolished what was left of the house and rebuilt it. The new edifice was not built exactly on the foundation of the former house, but more to the north, and nearer the Green Park, facing east. It covered part of the Mulberry Gardens and some of the ground which belonged to the Crown; this was to have repercussions.

Henry Wise, the greatest gardener of the day, was called in to improve the grounds, and he laid out a formal garden to the north of the new house, undertaking to level this ground for £1,000. Plantations of limes were set, and a planted-out parterre was planned, and room made for a sunk lawn or bowling green. This was a typical English garden feature of the period, and to this day a sunk lawn, with sloping sides, is known in France as a 'boulingrin'.

Lord Mulgrave was a remarkable man. He had been an admirer of the future Queen Anne, and had even aspired to marry her. He was a poet, dashing, and an experienced lover. It is not unlikely that the Princess was pleased at his attentions, for though the romance was doomed from the start, Mulgrave retained the affections of the sentimental Anne for the rest of his life.

Was his courtship motivated by ambitions, as some of Lord Mulgrave's biographers have suggested? He was already the favourite of King Charles, who had loaded him with honours '. . . and it is a moot point whether he would have braved what he, of all people, must have known would be the King's displeasure, unless there was a very strong impulse – one stronger than ambition – urging him forward to trespass on such dangerous ground . . .' Thus Bruce Graeme, and one

The crest of Henry Wise, gardener to Queen Anne: 'a demy-lion argent holding a damask rose, stalked and seeded proper'.

John Sheffield, Duke of Buckingham (1648–1721). As a young man, he was a suitor for Queen Anne and remained a favourite of hers all his life. He rebuilt Arlington House, facing east, as Buckingham Palace does today. By Godfrey Kneller.

would like to think that he is right.

Whatever Lord Mulgrave's motives in making love to Anne, retribution followed. He was stripped of all his offices; and there is an almost incredible story that, when he volunteered to go on a naval expedition to recapture Tangiers from the Moors, he was especially assigned to a leaky ship, which was unlikely to weather rough seas. That the good-natured Charles II should

Queen Anne (1665–1714) made her old admirer Duke of Buckingham, and gave him 'Two rods and nine perches' of her Royal Park of St James, but the Duke took more, which led to a quarrel in 1703.

OPPOSITE
One of the side rooms of the Garden Pavilion was decorated in the Pompeian taste (*see chapter* XII)

try to drown one of his favourite courtiers, and all his shipmates, just because he had made up to a Royal Princess, surpasses belief. But the story was current at the time, and has been often retold.

If there was a plot, it certainly miscarried. The ship survived the voyage, Tangiers was retaken, and Mulgrave returned a hero: the King forgave him.

In spite of his affection for the Stuarts and Princess Anne in particular, with the arrival of William III, Mulgrave changed sides with the best of them such as the future Duke of Marlborough, half the nobility of England and Princess Anne herself, and he was rewarded by Dutch William with a Marquisate.

On the accession of Queen Anne in 1702, he really came into his own. Anne had by no means forgotten her old admirer, and within a year of her accession she made him a Duke, whether of Buckingham or Buckinghamshire it has never quite been established. But if he was made Duke of Buckinghamshire he surely would have named his new house differently, for when he bought Arlington House, and rebuilt it, he firmly renamed it Buckingham House.

The Duke of Buckingham's politics, always devious, have little bearing on this book, unlike, to some extent, his building activities, and to a very great extent his gardening ones.

The purchase, some years before, of the Crow Fields had considerably enlarged the property to the north-west of Buckingham House. To this, for her new Duke, Queen Anne added a small slice of St James's Park itself . . . 'two rods and nine perches'.

But the self-confident Buckingham helped himself to more Crown land, and built his new house on the main axis of St James's Park, with its avenues and canal. In fact, he located it in such a way that it looked as if the whole Park was his own domain. This was too much even for the indulgent Anne who on 23rd August 1703, had the following sharp note sent to the Surveyor General of Crown Lands, at that time, Samuel Travers.

'The Queen notes that the Duke of Buckingham, upon rebuilding his house, hath gone further into the Park than he had leave from the Queen to do. You are to write to him that Her Majesty expects him to comply with the leave given him, which, as Her Majesty has declared, was only to take in a ditch,

and a little beyond a tree, before his said house, so as there might be a straight line.'

But the Duke took little notice, and the location of his new house remained unchanged, and very magnificent it looked. In 1708 the New View of London described it as 'a graceful palace . . . not to be contemned by the greatest monarch', and another writer, Robert Seymour, * though he held that there were more beautiful houses in London, praised Buckingham House on account of its 'situation, and the liberty it allows the spectator of seeing it from whatever point of view he pleases'.

There exists several telling descriptions of Buckingham House but 'the first of all these, in intimacy, correctness and style, is the famous narration of the owner himself'.† This takes the form of a letter as 'a graphic sketch' and considers that 'it would be an incomplete history which does not include the epistle'. But as our particular history is about the gardens, rather than about the house, emphasis will be placed on those parts of the Duke's letter which deal with the outside, rather than the inside of his 'graceful palace'.

> Visits after a certain hour are not to be avoided, some of which I own a little fatiguing (though thanks to the town's laziness they come pretty late) if the gardens were not so near, as to give a seasonable refreshment between those ceremonious interruptions. And I am more sorry than my coachman myself, if I am forced to go abroad any part of the morning. For though my garden as such, by not pretending to rarities or curiosities, has nothing in it to inveigh [sic] one's thoughts, yet by the advantage of situation and prospect, it is able to suggest the noblest that can be, in presenting at once to view a vast Town, a Palace, and a magnificent Cathedral. I confess the last with all its splendour, has less share in exciting my devotion than the most common snail in my garden. For though I am apt to be sincerely devout in any sort of religious assemblies, from the very best (that of our own Church) even to those of Jews, Turks and Indians, yet the works of nature appear to me the better sort of sermons, and every flower contains in it the most edifying rhetorick to fill us with admiration of its omnipotent Creator.

*Pseudonym for John Mottley (1692–1750)   †Bruce Graeme

OPPOSITE
A picture taken in early spring. One of the leafless trees is a contorted Sweet Chestnut (*Castanea sativa*) which may have begun life as a Bonsai (*see page 96*).

Buckingham House in 1754. The east façade looking down what is now The Mall. Above the door was a gilded inscription *'Sic siti laetantur lares'* 'the household gods delight in such a situation'.

(*Below*) The magnificent view to the east. By realigning his new house, and encroaching a little on St James's Park, the Duke of Buckingham contrived to make The Mall look like his own avenue.

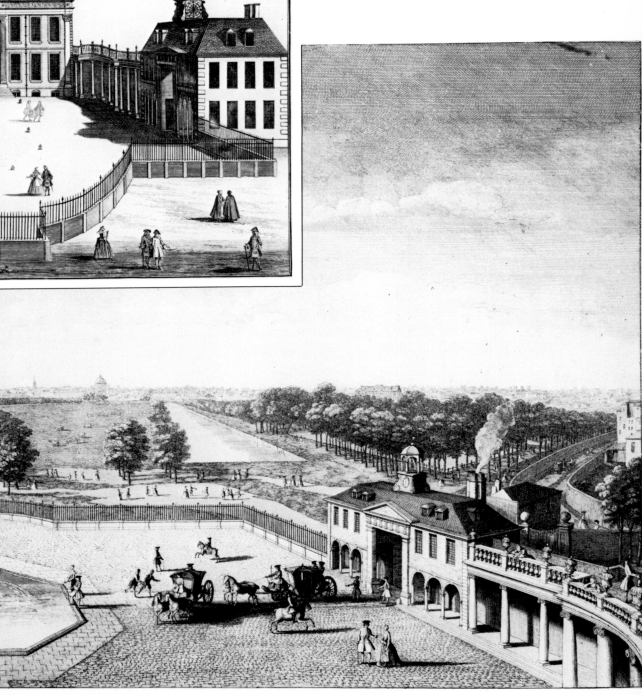

In a later part of his letter, the Duke describes the view from the windows on the east side of the house.

> The Avenues to the house are along St. James's Park, through rows of godly elms on one hand and gay flourishing limes on the other, that for coaches, this for walking; with the Mall lying between them. This reaches to my iron palisade that incompasses a square court, which has in its midst a great bason with statues and water works, and from its entrance, rises all the way imperceptibly till we mount to a Terrace in the front of a large Hall, paved with square white stones mixed with a dark-coloured marble, the walls of it covered with a sett [sic] of pictures done in the school of Raphael.

After an elaborate guided tour through the inside of his palace – for palace it already was, if not yet in name – statue by statue, and cabinet by cabinet, the Duke takes the impressed visitor to the roof, where

> . . . a leaden cistern, holding fifty tuns of water, driven up by an engine from the Thames, supplies all the water-works in the courts and gardens, which lie quite round the house, through one of which a grass walk conducts to the stables, built round a court, with six coach houses and 40 stalls.

Finally he reaches the garden, to which

> we go down from the house by seven steps, into a gravel walk that reaches across the whole garden, with a covered arbour at each end of it. Another of 30 foot broad leads from the front of the house, and lies between two groves of tall lime trees planted in several equal ranks upon a carpet of grass: the outsides of these groves are bordered with tubs of Bays and Orange-trees.
>
> At the end of this broad walk, you go up to a Terrace 400 paces long, with a large Semicircle in the middle, from whence is beheld the Queen's two parks, and a

great part of Surrey; then going down a few steps you walk on the banks of a canal 600 yards long, and 17 broad, with two rows of limes on each side.

On one side of this Terrace a Wall covered with Roses and Jassemines is made low to admit the view of a meadow full of cattle just under it, (no disagreeable object in the midst of a great city) and at each end a descent into parterres with fountains and water-works. From the biggest of these parterres we pass into a little square garden that has a fountain in the middle, and two green houses on the sides, with a convenient bathing apartment in one of them; and near another part of it lies a flower garden. Below all this, a kitchen-garden full of the best sorts of fruit, has several walks in it fit for the coldest weather.

Thus I have done with a tedious description: Only one thing I forgot, 'tis the little closet of Books at the end of that green-house which besides their being so very near, are ranked in such a method, that by its mark, a very Irish footman may fetch any book I want. Under the windows of this closet and green-house is a little wilderness full of black birds and nightingales. The Trees, though planted by myself, require lopping already, to prevent their hindering the view of that fine canal in the Park.

The touch of having his favourite books 'ranked' in such a way that even 'a very Irish' footman could find them, is particularly pleasing.

On each façade of the house, the scholarly Duke affixed elegant Latin inscriptions in letters of gold. To the east, and visible in the illustration on pages 34–5: SIC SITI LAETANTUR – 'The Household Gods delight in such a situation' – as plainly His Grace did too: and on the garden side, more obviously: RUS IN URBE.

The Duke of Buckingham died in 1721 and left the house, its splendid contents and the garden to his wife who was such a character that she deserves some pages to herself.

VI

'Princess Buckingham'

The funeral effigy of 'Princess Buckingham' in Westminster Abbey. Inordinately proud of her half-royal descent 'her chief anxiety on her death bed was that her waiting women might take the liberty of sitting down in her presence before she had actually expired'.

Catherine, Duchess of Buckingham was a natural daughter of James II by Catherine Sedley, herself the natural daughter of the playwright Sir Charles Sedley who has already figured in this narrative. When she was born, her Royal father, with more imagination than he usually showed, gave her the name of Darnley, presumably after Mary, Queen of Scots' unfortunate husband, and his own great-grandfather. Her mother, Catherine Sedley, was remarkably plain. But she was a wit, and when asked how she could have captured the affections of James, she confessed her ignorance. 'It cannot be for my beauty,' she said, 'because I have none. And it cannot be for my wit, for he has not enough to appreciate it.'

Catherine Darnley married the Duke of Buckingham as her third husband, and was so ridiculously proud of her half Royal parentage that she became something of a joke — her servants wore the Royal liveries (when they were not in mourning for the Stuarts), and Horace Walpole jibed at her as Princess Buckingham. Her chief anxiety on her death-bed was that her waiting women might take the liberty of sitting down in her presence before she had actually expired. By the Duke, she had two sons. One died in childhood, the second Edmund, second Duke of Buckingham, was an invalid, and a shadowy but rather appealing figure. He died in Rome while he was still a youth. He must have had happy childhood memories of the garden at Buckingham House, as he left in his will a request that he might be buried there 'in that field next to the terras, where a little modest tomb might be erected, covered over with a small open Temple'.

The simple request did not at all suit Princess Buckingham and Edmund ended up in a pompous sarcophagus in Westminster Abbey.

In 1723, the Prince of Wales (afterwards George II) cast his eye on Buckingham House and endeavoured to buy it. A letter exists in which the proud Duchess set out her terms. At the time she was described as bargaining 'with the haughtiness of a Jacobite and the astuteness of an Estate Agent'.

If their Royal Highnesses will have everything stand as it does, furniture and pictures, I will have £3,000 per annum, both run hazard of being spoiled, and the last, to be sure, will be all to be new bought whenever my son is of age. The quantity the rooms take cannot be well furnished under £10,000; but if their Highnesses will permit the pictures all to be removed and buy the furniture as it will be valued by different people, the

An extract from an inventory taken of the contents of the house and garden in 1743, in the Sheffield family archives. Such delicate plants as lemon trees and aloes and oleanders figure on the list.

The Green Houses

12 Pyramid Bays, 1 Large Amd Aloe, 3 Middle Size do, 4 Small do, 5 Oleanders in Pots, 1 Large Cutysons in a Tub, 39 Small do in Pots, 17 Mirtels in Pots 4 Span Jefso 16 Munnums Tree Wormwood 1 Geranium a Cypress in a Pot 2 large Lemons in Tubs 3 Large Cytrons in Tubs, 21 Large Orange Trees, in Large Tubs a Do, a Stock in a large Tub, 26 Middle Size in Tubs 10 Cytrons in Large Pots, 12 Small do & Lemons in Pots, 27 Oranges in Pots, 6 Small Do in Pots, 63 Small Orange Stocks in Pots 2 Tythimal in Pots Stands & 2 old Water Tubs 107. 0. 0

A hitherto unpublished picture, in the possession of the Sheffield family, showing the west side of Buckingham House and the garden. The picture is neither signed nor dated, but as Westminster Abbey is shown without its west towers, started by Hawksmoor in 1732 and not completed for thirteen years, it must date from before 1745. The track with a coach and horsemen follows much the same line as Constitution Hill.

house shall go at £2,000 – If the Prince and Princess prefer the buying outright, under £60,000 it will not be parted with as it now stands, and all His Majesty's revenue cannot purchase a place so fit for them nor for a less sum – The Princess asked me at the Drawing Room if I would sell my fine house. I answered her smiling, that I was under no necessity to part with it; yet, when what I thought was the value of it should be offered, perhaps my prudence might overcome my inclination.

Her terms were not accepted, and she was to live in the house for the rest of her life.

At last, in 1742, Horace Walpole wrote 'Princess Buckingham is dead or dying', and Buckingham House and all its

contents passed to a natural son of the late Duke, Charles Herbert, on condition he took his father's family name of Sheffield. From Charles Sheffield descends the large and distinguished family of Sheffield today. One, the late Major Reginald Sheffield, was a close friend of mine. At his house in Yorkshire and in his family, there are many pieces of furniture and pictures which came from Buckingham House, among which is an unusual view of the building from the garden side as it was in the early 18th century and never before published. It is shown on page 40.

Perhaps Charles Sheffield, so newly translated to vast wealth, found living in Buckingham House too overpowering, for in 1761 he sold it to the Crown, and Buckingham House became the property of George III, the direct ancestor of all the Kings and Queens of England who have since occupied it.

Buckingham House and garden in 1760. It is interesting to compare with the plan on page 26. Crace collection.

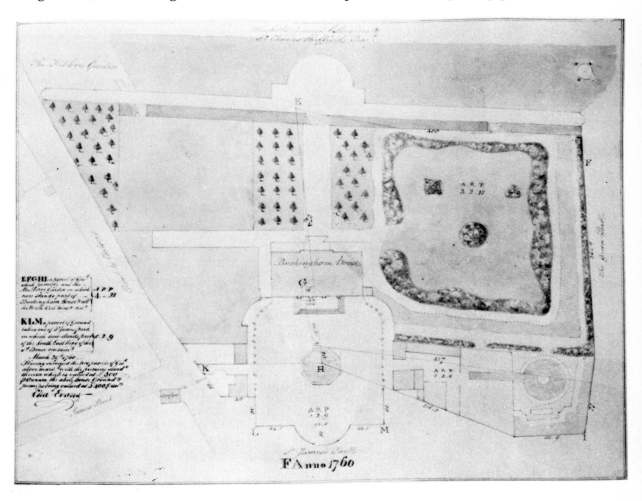

VII

Buckingham House becomes the Queen's House

George III succeeded to the throne while still unmarried in 1760. His bride, Princess Charlotte of Mecklenberg-Strelitz, was plain, but she had charm, and she was to be a model wife. She bore her husband fifteen children, fourteen of whom were to be born within the red brick walls of the Queen's House, as Buckingham House was soon to be rechristened in her honour.

The object of King George's purchase of Buckingham House was to escape from the formality of life in St James's Palace, and to find a home, elegant and large enough to be a Royal residence, but where the King and Queen, who both were innately simple people, could lead a comfortable domestic life, alone with their growing family.

Even the sometimes spiteful Horace Walpole approved the move. 'I cannot help telling you how comfortable the new disposition of the Court is to me. The King and his wife are settled for good and all at Buckingham House: and are stripping the other palaces to furnish it . . . they have already fetched pictures from Hampton Court, which indicate their never living there.'

Like all owners of a new house, King George embarked on alterations which were sometimes criticised – especially by John Noorthouk, who likened the addition of stables, wash houses and a hen roost to the accretions which might grow up round a country parsonage. But there is no record of these new buildings affecting the garden and it can be taken that the gardens, for the time at least, remained as they had been described by the Duke of Buckingham in the letter already quoted.

By 6th June 1763, the alterations inside were promised to be complete, and Queen Charlotte had the idea of devising a pleasant surprise for her husband's birthday. As every Etonian knows, King George's birthday was on the 4th June. On this particular year he was persuaded not only to postpone the celebrations until the 6th, but to move back to St James's

King George III (1738–1820) and Queen Charlotte. They were a homely couple, and added wash houses and a hen roost to the amenities of The Queen's House. Queen Charlotte delighted in growing carnations.

Palace for a few of the preceeding days so that Queen Charlotte's designs could go ahead in secrecy.

On the night of the 6th the King returned and was at once conducted to a window overlooking the garden. There a dazzling spectacle, lit by four thousand lights, met his gratified gaze. A temple and bridge had been conjured for the night, and an immense painting of King George himself giving peace to all parts of the earth. (The war of American Independence was still ten years away.) The King was reported as 'highly delighted with this unexpected testimony of his Consort's love and respect' and it is to be hoped that the damage to the lawns and plantations of the garden was not too severe.

The happily married King and Queen delighted in walking in the garden which, it must be remembered, at that time merged at the western end with the fields and orchards of what was later to become Belgravia. But London was growing fast, and soon there were proposals to build a line of large houses – the present Grosvenor Place – which would overlook the garden to the west. Alarmed at the thought of this loss of privacy, King George asked the Government to buy the land, but the Treasury was unwilling to spend the £20,000 that was needed, and the chance was missed.

The sense of being overlooked was, in the course of time, to cause the King and Queen to fall out of love with Buckingham House, and to transfer their affections to Windsor and Kew. But that was to be in the future, when King George was suffering from his increasingly severe mental attacks. In the sixties and early seventies their delight, and particularly Queen Charlotte's, in their new home was unalloyed, especially when, in 1775, Buckingham House became Queen Charlotte's own property, by Act of Parliament. From then on, for half a century, it was officially known as the Queen's House.

The garden played a role in the five anxious days of the anti-Roman Catholic Gordon Riots in 1780. Dickens sets the scene in his inimitable way in *Barnaby Rudge*, and describes the destruction of the Earl of Mansfield's house, and how the mob had called on those within to open the door:

> . . . and receiving no reply [for Lord and Lady Mansfield were at that moment escaping by the

backway] forced an entrance according to their usual custom. That they then began to demolish the house with great fury, and setting fire to it in several parts, involved in a common ruin the whole of the costly furniture, the plate and jewels, a beautiful gallery of pictures, the rarest collection of manuscripts ever possessed by any one private person in the world, and worse than all, because nothing could replace this loss, the great Law Library, on almost every page of which were notes in the Judge's own hand, of inestimable value – being the results of the study and experience of his whole life . . .

That night houses of well known Roman Catholics burned all over London, and the crowd roamed unchecked through the streets destroying and looting as they went. But next day strong measures were taken and, Dickens records, '. . . at the Queen's palace, a double guard, the yeomen on duty, the groom-porters, and all other attendants, were stationed in the passages and on the staircases at seven o'clock, with strict

The Gordon Riots, 1780. 'The crowd roamed unchecked through the streets, destroying and looting as they went . . .' An illustration by 'Phiz', Hablot Browne from Dickens' *Barnaby Rudge*. During the riots, troops were stationed in the gardens of The Queen's House.

instructions to be watchful on their posts all night'; All the doors were locked. Several thousand troops were stationed in the garden, while the officers were quartered in the Riding School. The King took the greatest interest in their welfare, and on discovering that the soldiers had no bedding – not even straw to lie on – he made them a cheering speech, beginning, 'My lads, my crown cannot purchase you straw tonight, but depend upon it . . . a sufficiency will be here tomorrow'. Meanwhile he regaled them with wine and spirits, and kept them company himself through the night. The next day, the mob dispersed and the crisis passed.

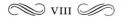

VIII

Queen Charlotte

Queen Charlotte is not generally thought of as a botanist – but she had a keen interest in plants and trees; and her patronage of horticulture was recognised when the Reverend Charles Abbot dedicated a book to her in 1798, and described her, with only slight exaggeration, as 'the first female Botanist in the wide circle of the British Dominions'. This was in the dedication of his *Flora Bedfordiensis*. Twenty years before this, the Queen had had a flower named after her and her native Strelitz, *Strelitzia reginae*, and Sir Joseph Banks paid her this graceful compliment: 'A just tribute of respect to the botanical zeal and knowledge of the present Queen of England.'

The strelitzia, still called, colloquially, the Queen Flower Plant, or Bird of Paradise Flower, is a popular hot house plant, and still widely grown. Its exotic orange and blue petals and curiously shaped flower were illustrated in Sydenham Edwards's beautiful book *The New Botanic Garden*, published in 1812, while Henry James Pye, author of many Royal birthday odes, well-meaning but tedious, and Poet Laureate from 1790 to 1813, composed the following verse in the strelitzia's honour:

> Graced by Her name, its shining petals boast
>   Above the rest, to charm Her favouring eyes
> Though Flora brings from every clime her host
>   Of various odours and of varied dyes.

Olwen Hedley, in her masterly biography of Queen Charlotte tells us that William Townsend Aiton, who had succeeded his father as chief gardener at Kew, acknowledged Queen Charlotte's continued patronage, in his *Deliniations of Exotick Plants . . . . . in the royal garden at Kew . . .* which he published in 1796 (–1805). No event, he said, 'had so materially tended to the increase of the Royal Collection [at Kew] as that

Gillofloure as drawn for Gerard's *Herball* (1597).

OPPOSITE
Drifts of crocus carpet the turf below a grove of commemorative trees. In the foreground, an Indian Chestnut (*Aesculus indica*) planted by King George VI to mark the Coronation in 1937.

decided preference which our most gracious Queen has of late condescended to bestow upon the Science of Botany'. And Robert Thornton records that the Queen had drawn many of the plants in the collection at Kew 'which contains all the choicest productions of the habitable globe.'

Queen Charlotte also indulged in the hobby, so popular in her day, of collecting dried and pressed flowers, and some remnants of her collection have come to rest in the Herbarium at the Royal Botanic Gardens at Kew. Olwen Hedley writes touchingly '. . . few people ask to see it, but to turn the loose sheets on which the withered specimens are mounted, is to become aware of the patient striving, the modest quest for scientific truth, and the dedicated talent of the Queen.'

I am indebted to Miss Jean Bowden of the Herbarium at Kew for the full story of Queen Charlotte's collection of pressed plants. This was originally made by the botanist John Lightfoot, author of *Flora Scotica* who, according to Sir James Edward Smith, in *Rees Cyclopedia* Vol. 21, published in 1819:

> . . . had, in the course of his botanical studies, collected an excellent British herbarium, consisting of abundant specimens, generally gathered wild, and in many cases important for the illustration of his work [*Flora Scotica*]. He also amassed, from Sir Joseph Banks and other friends, a number of exotic plants. The whole was bought, after his death, for 100 guineas, by His Majesty [George III] as a present to the queen and deposited at Frogmore, the price being fixed by an intelligent friend of the family. The specimens having been for some time neglected, were, after a while, discovered to be much infested with insects; and as their royal possessor, having a genuine and ardent taste for the study of botany, was anxious for their preservation, the writer of the present article was requested to give his advice and assistance on this subject. This led to his [Sir J. E. Smith's] frequent invitation as a visitor at Frogmore, and to a regular course of conversations, rather than lectures, on botany and zoology, which Her Majesty, and the Princesses Augusta and Elizabeth, honoured with their diligent attention; the queen regularly taking notes of every lecture, which she read over

ÆSCULUS
INDICA
PLANTED BY
H. M.
KING GEORGE VI
TO COMMEMORATE
THE CORONATION
1937

aloud at its conclusion, to prevent mistakes. The plan of this exemplary mother, on which she has often been heard to descant, was, in the education of her royal offspring, to open as many resources to them as possible, in a variety of studies and pursuits; out of which they might subsequently make their own choice, and thus be independent of circumstances for occupation and amusement.

But we have strayed from the garden of the Queen's House to the garden at Kew, as King George III and Queen Charlotte were so often to do.

With London growing up all round it, and the new houses of Belgravia peering over the wall (if wall there was at that time: the present wall is on record of having been built in the 1830s), the Queen's House was to lose its early charm. Soon there are more and more references in the Queen's correspondence to 'Dear Kew' where it seems they lived 'very retired'. Kew the Queen found 'uncommonly cheerful', and in a letter to her brother in Germany – written in a curious French – describing the time the Queen passed there, she writes, *'Ce séjour est très de mon goût, vue que nous y vivons très retiri . . . nous amusons aise'.*

King George, in particular, had come to dislike London, and wrote, 'In Summer, a box sent to the Queen's House is less likely to meet [me] than at any other place, for I certainly see as little of London as I possibly can, and am never a volunteer there'.

However, one of the lasting pleasures that the spreading grounds of the Queen's House in London afforded the King and Queen, were the exotic animals they were able to keep there: and in the intervals of cultivating her favourite carnations, and resting during her many pregnancies in her garden-tent, Queen Charlotte could stroll over to the part of the grounds now covered by Buckingham Palace Road, and visit the paddock reserved for 'the Queen's animals'. Among these was a bad tempered zebra, and an elephant – and in those days before the London Zoo they became 'one of the sights . . . especially as attendants added to the exotic interest'. These were two East Indians, Senetel, in a rose lustrine Turkish robe, and his assistant Newran, in a chintz cotton mantle. *

The curious, hardly identifiable bird – half ostrich and half

Queen Charlotte by Olwen Hedley: John Murray 1975

OPPOSITE
Daffodils and the new avenue of *Aesculus indica* planted to give some privacy from high-rise buildings.

49

Queen Charlotte and her two eldest sons – by Zoffany – painted about 1767, with an oblique view of the garden. *Reproduced by gracious permission of Her Majesty the Queen.*

cassowary – which is seen through the window straying on the lawn in Zoffany's delightful portrait of Queen Charlotte at her dressing table – was certainly one of the collection. In this portrait, painted about 1767, there is an oblique view of the garden through the open window. It tells us little of how it looked, but one can see a stretch of lawn and part of a formally clipped hedge – probably of yew. It is likely that the garden, throughout Queen Charlotte's occupation of the Queen's House, retained much of the formality which had been fashionable in the Duke of Buckingham's day. Queen Charlotte was not a great innovator and, in any case, her affection for her London residence had been weaned away by the pastoral delights of Kew, where the King's mother – Princess Augusta, a serious botanist – had recently founded what was to become the most famous botanical garden in the world.

It was George IV, who succeeded to the throne in 1820, who was to transform, not only the Queen's House, which he lost no time in renaming Buckingham Palace (The King's House and The Pimlico Palace, had been considered as alternative names), but also the garden. Most of the old Buckingham House was pulled down and rebuilt at enormous public expense, and the garden was radically remodelled.

The present garden of Buckingham Palace lies to the west of the Palace itself, and occupies the area once known as the Crow Fields. In a plan of the garden at Buckingham House dated 1743, an area near the house is shown as being formally laid out, and it is known that Queen Anne's gardener, Henry Wise, had a hand in the embellishment of the grounds.

But, until the coming of George IV, no attempt had been made to landscape the whole area. This was now done, in the 'natural' style, by William Townsend Aiton (1766–1849), son of the garden manager at Kew (whom he had succeeded in 1793), and the protégé of George IV's grandmother, Augusta, Princess of Wales. 'Besides being a great botanist,' Clifford Smith tells us, the younger Aiton 'had studied the fashionable art of landscape gardening . . .'

IX

The Garden is Landscaped

The Landscape Garden, it has been said, is the most important contribution that the British have made to Art. And it is true that nowhere in the world is the art of landscape gardening so well understood as in England. By 1820, of course, it was no longer a new idea. Nearly a century before, William Kent had transformed the garden at Rousham, sweeping away its formal hedges, fountains and statues, and replaced them with grass and thoughtfully-sited groups of trees. Part of Kent's early career had been spent in Italy, and on his return, his head full of memories of the classical paintings of Claude and Salvator Rosa, 'he sought to recreate their sunlit landscapes in his native land . . . he was in the forefront of the revolt against the artificiality of seventeenth century garden-design'.

Kent was followed by Lancelot (Capability) Brown, a far more famous name than Kent in the history of landscape gardening in Britain. (Brown achieved his sobriquet of Capability from his customary opening remark on being shown a possible new assignment: 'Let us study the capabilities of the site'.) But Kent it was who first 'leaped the fence, and saw that all Nature was a garden' as Horace Walpole aptly put it. Kent died in 1748, and Brown in 1783.

William Aiton was a latecomer in the field, but he was certainly much influenced by his greater predecessors: under his direction the whole Palace garden quickly took on the look of a natural park which Kent and Capability Brown had made the fashion a hundred years before. The theory of natural gardening had been epitomized long before, in verse, by Alexander Pope, and Aiton was one of its disciples.

> To build, to plant, whatever you intend,
> To rear the column, or the arch to bend,
> To swell the terrase, or to sink the Grot;
> In all, let Nature never be forgot.

But treat the goddess like a modest fair,
Nor over-dress, nor leave her wholly bare;
Let not each beauty ev'ry where be spy'd
Where half the skill is decently to hide:
He gains all points, who pleasingly confounds,
Surprizes, varies, and conceals the Bounds.

Consult the genius of the place in all:
That tells the Waters or to rise, or fall,
Or helps th'ambitious Hill the heav'n to scale,
Or scoops in circling Theatres the Vale,
Calls in the country, catches opening glades,
Joins willing woods, and varies shades with shades,
Now breaks, or now directs, th'intending Lines,
Paints as you plant, and as you work, designs.

John Nash (1752–1835) George IV's favourite architect; a miniature in wax by J. Couriguer. Though derided in his lifetime, and for some years after his death, Nash's reputation now stands high. He was the architect of the splendid west façade of the Palace, of old Regent Street and the Regent's Park Terraces.

'In all let NATURE never be forgot . . .' that is the key line in Pope's verse, and Aiton marked it well. Nash's 'terrase' swelled but, by judicious planting of groups of trees in the Brunonian style, Aiton successfully concealed the bounds. Many of the fine trees which add so much to the beauty of the Royal garden today were planted by Aiton.

One of his more spectacular developments in the garden of George IV's new Palace was the transformation of two small ponds into the impressive lake which is now such a feature of the garden. This is shaped like a large letter S without the bottom curl; when it was excavated, the earth removed was used to make the mound which runs along the south side of the garden. This was then planted with trees to make an efficient screen between the garden of the Palace and Buckingham Palace Road and the Royal Stables. But as the lake is nowhere deeper than six feet, and the mound is, for all its length, at least 25 feet high, some mystery exists as to where the soil used to construct it came from.

With the public the mound was unpopular from the start, and in 1832 there was a complaint about it in the House of Commons when it was described as 'going up by contract in the garden, from the rubbish and filth brought in from all parts of the town'. All through the 19th century, soil was added to the mound from Hyde Park (perhaps when the Dell was excavated?), from Shirley Common, and from Norwood. As

Nash's much ridiculed east façade of
the Palace.

An imaginary view of the garden with
its new embellishments.

Nash and a fair companion at the base
of The Mound.

'. . . The Pyramids, Temples and
Ditches, Where Naiads and Cupids are
seen without breeches.'

George IV and his giraffe.

About 1826 – when George IV had been on the throne for six years, an unkind skit was published by Hume called 'the palace that N–H built' one verse of which is included in the text. The story of the giraffe which features in the illustrations is an interesting one. The giraffe had been an unusual present to the King from Mohammed Ali, Pasha of Egypt. Its history was as follows. Some of Mohammed Ali's soldiers had surprised two young giraffes grazing on the plains of Senaar. They shot the mother and sold the young animals to the local Governor who, in turn, presented them to Mohammed Ali. One of the young giraffes was strong and healthy – the other less so. Mohammed Ali decided that the giraffes would make handsome presents for the Kings of England and France respectively, and approached the Consuls of the two countries, who tossed up (or whatever Consuls do) to decide which King got what. The British Consul lost, and the weaker of the two young giraffes was dispatched to England. Its arrival occasioned intense public interest, and dozens of cartoons appeared making the usual unkind fun of George IV and his new pet. However, though doted on by the King and cossetted by its keepers, the poor animal only survived two years and, on its death the *Windsor and Eton Express* published the sad news that 'Messrs Gould and Thompson, of the Zoological Gardens were about to dissect the body.'

Charles X's giraffe, on the other hand, lived for eighteen years, equally cossetted, and occasionally fed on rose-leaves by the French monarch in person.

recently as 1961, when the Cascade was constructed, good turves were brought from Essex as well as good top soil from Kent. In 1840 Prince Albert, Queen Victoria's artistic consort, conjured a series of gravel paths on the much-discussed mound. Prince Albert's efforts to embellish the garden were apparently necessary, as a contemporary note recorded that the garden was '. . . destitute of the customary interesting appearance of a flower garden'. In 1844 the Prince made another attempt to give interest to the garden by building, on the top of the mound, an elegant little Pavilion decorated inside by the leading artists of the day. The story of this little building is interesting, and will be recounted later. Today, sadly, the paths on the mound and the Pavilion itself have disappeared: but on the credit side, the trees with which the mound was planted have reached maturity, and make a most effective screen.

Back to the lake: on a map of the garden of between 1795 and 1818, two ponds are marked, one sixty feet by twenty feet, one much smaller. These, as we have recorded, were replaced by Aiton at the command of George IV with the much larger lake which we see today. Work on Aiton's lake and mound (for he was responsible for that as well) was going on while John Nash (1752–1835) was busily employed rebuilding the Palace itself. Both came in for some unkind comment, and there is an illustrated skit in the British Museum Library, written by I. Hume about 1826, under the title of 'The palace that N – – H built', which runs:

King George IV (1820–30) by Isaac Cruickshank. By the time he became King, he had lost the great good looks and fine figure of his youth. But Buckingham Palace, and especially its gardens, owe him a great debt.

> This is the large Pond of Water or Bason
> Where the Royal Narcissus may see his dear face in,
> E'er he rove 'mong the Pyramids, Temples and Ditches
> Where Naiads and Cupids are seen without breeches
> Who preside o'er the Fountains, the Promenades and Rides
> Which lead up to the Hill, the magnificent Mound,
> Thrown up in the garden, full half a mile round,
> Thickly planted with trees, and as high as a steeple
> To protect from the breeze and to hide from the people

'To hide from the people . . .' By 1825 Poor Prinny had lost the great good looks and fine figure he had had when he was called

The First Gentleman of Europe, and the radical M.P. Lord Folkestone made the unkind joke, that 'he had finally let loose his belly'. Towards the end of his reign as George IV, he was shy of appearing in public, and led a life (mostly at Windsor) of almost complete seclusion. For in the gentler words of Max Beerbohm, 'In reality the King was now too fat by far' to brook the observation of casual eyes. Especially 'he hated to be seen by those whose memories might bear them back to the time when he yet had a waist'.

George IV
and William IV

While the lake was being enlarged and shelter belts of trees planted, Aiton busied himself with doing away with the last remnants of the Duke of Buckingham's formal garden.

Below the terrace which Nash had laid along the whole length of the new west façade, a vast area of grass was cleared, making the lawn much as it exists today. The lake was finally finished by 1828 – two years before George IV died – and was referred to as the Fish Pond. The water to fill it came, via a reservoir which stood near the site of the present Constitution Hill Arch, by underground conduits from the Serpentine. By cutting a promontory, an island was formed by about 1835. There was no bridge until 1841. Records of the garden at this period are scanty, but the industrious Prince Albert may well have been responsible for this useful addition.

Work on the garden was still going on when the King died in 1830 and was succeeded by his brother William IV.

No record is available of what King George's alterations to the garden had cost, but in rebuilding the Palace, Nash had spent over £600,000. Compton Mackenzie exonerates the King when he writes: 'The blame for this rests more heavily on the different ministries than upon George IV, and his favourite architect . . .' But George IV was wildly extravagant, and his natural good taste, if at times a trifle bizarre, and his very real sense of the dignity of the Monarch (at least in so far as to how he was housed) can hardly excuse his enormous outlay of public money. When he died, Buckingham Palace and all it stood for, had got itself a bad name.

William IV, a sailor of the simplest tastes, at first refused flatly to move in. He disliked grandeur and pomposity in any form: for years, as Duke of Clarence, he had lived at Bushey House – a large house in Middlesex, surrounded by spreading grounds. There, while engendering a vast family of illegitimate Fitzclarences by his amiable and talented mistress, the actress

Dorothy Jordan, he had gardened and farmed and generally lived the life of a country gentleman.

After the unexpected death in 1817, in childbirth, of the heiress to the throne, George IV's daughter Princess Charlotte, it became clear to all that Sailor William one day would be King. Dorothy Jordan was unloaded, and the Duke was suitably married to a German Princess, Adelaide, and set about preparing to mount the throne. But he remained simple in his tastes, and disapproved not only of his brother, the King's, way of life but also of his elaborate taste in houses.

As soon as he succeeded in 1830 he at once began thinking of reasons not to move into Buckingham Palace. First he suggested that it might make an admirable barracks for the Foot Guards. But the offer was refused by Lord Grey on account of the expense, and King William had reluctantly to sanction the building of Wellington Barracks in Birdcage Walk where the iron railings still bear his cypher, W IV.

Then, when the Houses of Parliament were burned down in 1834, he seized the opportunity of offering Buckingham Palace to take their place, with the words: 'It would be the finest thing in Europe', adding 'Mind you, I mean it as a personal gift.' Lord Melbourne, the Home Secretary, was not attracted by the idea, and contrived that the accommodating architect Edward Blore should write a report pointing out the unsuitability of the building for such a purpose. 'Dexterously,' writes Philip Ziegler in his admirable biography of Melbourne, 'Lord Melbourne argued the perils of transferring Parliament to a more roomy site . . . "It will be very difficult to avoid providing much larger accommodation for spectators as well as members, and Lord Melbourne need not recall to Your Majesty, the fatal effect which large galleries filled with the multitude have had on the deliberations of public assemblies".'

The Sailor King still jibbed at the idea of living in the Palace which he found far too large and too ornate: it was not even shipshape. The doors did not fit, and the chimneys smoked. Above all, there was too much gilding, and King William had a passionate dislike for gilding. But before the fatal move was made, he died and was succeeded by his niece, Princess Victoria.

Within a few weeks of her accession, the young Queen visited Buckingham Palace and its garden, and decided that it would suit her very well. She walked round the garden and was pleased to record that her favourite spaniel Dashy was 'quite happy' in it. In due course her private apartments were redecorated, and the Queen was enchanted with them. 'It is all so changed, fresh painted and gilded: my rooms fresh painted, and the doors altered, and the ceiling gilt.' The youthful Queen Victoria did not seem to mind gilding at all.

∽ XI ∽

Queen Victoria

Queen Victoria (1819–1902) and Prince Albert (1819–1861) an engraving based on a painting by F. Winterhalter (1805–1873).

Throughout Queen Victoria's long reign of sixty-four years there are a few glimpses of the garden, but one feels that it did not play a great part in the life of the Royal Family. Here and there shafts of sunlight, warm and summery, clear and wintry, or dimmed by London mist, illumine the scene for a moment. But the moments are few, and passing.

In May 1841 the newly married Queen wrote to her Uncle, King Leopold of the Belgians: 'We have lovely weather . . . we sit out a great deal in this pretty and MOST INVALUABLE garden, which is so much improved, and sitting under the Lime Trees in the shade, with a pleasant breeze, is delicious.'[1]

Some years later, on February 22nd the Queen writes exuberantly: 'We have had very severe weather, which I delight in, as it agrees with me so well, and it brings with it so many cheerful amusements. The snow enabled the children to sledge down a bank [the mound?] like a MONTAGNE RUSSE . . . and the ice has been so strong and thick, that there has been delightful skaiting[sic].'[2]

The garden seems in those early years of her reign to have already the haunt of unexpected birds such as golden and silver pheasants, precursors of the flamingoes of today. In another letter to her uncle in Brussels the Queen reports 'no less than 81 pheasants eggs laid in our garden here. Is this not enormous? We have got, besides, 40 Silver Pheasant eggs laid, too.' In the same letter the Queen informs her uncle that the pheasant eggs have been sent to 'Grimm' at Claremont which was then still in King Leopold's possession, and the house near London where his wife, Princess Charlotte, had died. Grimm was bailiff there. * The Silver Pheasant eggs, presumably, the Queen kept for herself.

It is pleasant to recall the scenes in the garden in those idyllic early days of Queen Victoria's marriage with the meals out of doors, the lime trees scenting the air, the children playing on

Ornamental pheasants.

[1]Royal Archives Y90/21   [2]R.A. Y98/5   *R.A. Y91/49

61

'We have had very severe weather, which I delight in . . . and it brings with it so many cheerful amusements'. From a contemporary print.

the mound, and Prince Albert calling to his beloved greyhound Eos not to chase the pheasants. Eos after the rosy-fingered Greek goddess of the Dawn, whom the Romans called Aurora.

Prince Albert was interested in all the arts – far more so than the Queen, who wisely allowed her taste to be ruled entirely by her husband. In a speech at the opening of a Horticulture Show, the Prince Consort expressed himself with his usual good sense on the art of gardening. '. . . In this, the artist who lays out the work, and devises a garment for a piece of ground, has the delight of seeing his work live, and grow hour by hour; and, while it is growing, he is able to polish, to cut and carve, to fill up here and there, to hope and to love.'

In his too short life Prince Albert had little time to 'polish, cut and carve' in the garden of Buckingham Palace, though he did inspire the building of the Comus Pavilion. When he died

in 1861, darkness fell on the Palace and its garden. The Queen preferred to live out her widowhood at Windsor, Osborne or Balmoral. Buckingham Palace ceased to be loved, and was hardly ever occupied.

A dim light falls on the garden, and Queen Victoria's lingering affection for it, in 1881. It is shed by a correspondence in the Royal Archives at Windsor between Sir John Cowell, Master of the Household, Lord Sydney, Lord Steward, Mr Thomas, a garden designer of the day, and the Queen herself. In this correspondence the thinning out and replanting of the belt of trees along the Grosvenor Place wall, which was much overgrown, was discussed. A sensible and practical plan had been put forward for felling, soil renewal,

Queen Victoria's seat.

and replanting. But the Queen, when the work was well advanced, put a stop to it, and in a note in her own hand complained (like so many other garden owners have done before) that 'Mr Thomas always wants to alter and change – as he did at Sandringham. The Queen is very fond of the garden. It is beautifully laid out and extremely well kept. She only wants trees planted where they are dead, and the new ones planted near those that are dying off . . . she wants NO CHANGES.' So that was the end of that. *

Buckingham Palace may not have been a favourite home of Queen Victoria but, unconsciously, no doubt, she conferred an aura on the Palace for which it had waited through more than half a century of Royal occupation. She actually made it popular.

The Palace had been loathed by the public during the reign of George IV. It was thought, first and foremost, to have cost far too much. It had been personally disliked and, as it happened, had never been occupied by William IV. In the early days of Queen Victoria, such was the popularity of the young Queen, Buckingham Palace slightly gained ground in public esteem, but could still be the butt of humorists, as when the Queen wanted to enlarge it by adding the East Wing to accommodate her growing family. But Balmoral, Osborne and Windsor, in that order of preference, were Queen Victoria's favoured residences, and Buckingham Palace was a bad fourth. Then in 1861 her long widowhood started, and the Palace stood almost empty. After a few years, there was open criticism.

At last, after the Queen's two Jubilees, there was a change. From the dark, unknown building in the middle of London, Buckingham Palace suddenly became the heart of the Empire. It was the Queen who initiated Royal appearances on the famous balcony. A new bond was forged between the Monarch and the people and from that day, in times of joy and jubilee, of national crisis, of the illness and death of the wearer of the Crown, the eyes of the country have looked towards the Palace and for a few hours – or days – the hearts of the Sovereign and of the People beat as one. It was that great woman, Queen Victoria, who left this valuable legacy, as she did so many others, to our country.

---

*R.A. 1/140

The Waterloo Vase, made of one of the biggest single blocks of Carrara marble in the world (*see page 124*). Beyond, the high conical outline of a Swamp Cypress (*Taxodium distichum*) one of the most interesting trees in the garden (*see page 93*).

Camellias in early spring (*see chapter VII*).

XII

The Garden Pavilion

OPPOSITE
Magnolia soulangeana, with flowers flushed with pink.

(*Inset*) *Magnolia soulangeana* 'Picture' has upstanding white flowers dashed with purple.

As a rather lengthy postcript to the few foregoing glimpses of the garden at Buckingham Palace in Victorian times, the story of the Garden Pavilion must now be told. Though in its day it attracted a great deal of attention, very few people realize now that it ever existed. But it did, and in its way, it was unique.

First it must be affirmed that the early nineteenth century was hardly the heyday of romance in England. The rude blasts of the Industrial Revolution were blowing away the last shreds of the stylish fancies of the late Georgian age. Rococo and Chinoiserie were out of fashion. The harsh colour of the geranium had replaced the pale petals of the rose; and yet 'with 18th century tastes so much out of favour, it is almost startling

The Pavilion, built in 1844, has now disappeared. From the fly-leaf of Ludwig Grüner's book written by command of Queen Victoria in 1846, and now extremely rare.

Rosebud from the wallpaper of Queen Victoria's bedroom as a girl.

to find an occasion of elegant caprice in, of all unexpected places, the Buckingham Palace of the Queen and Prince Albert'. Thus wrote John Steegman in his scholarly book *Consort of Taste*. In 1844 the Queen, influenced, one can be sure, by her art-conscious husband, a pleasure dome decreed — in the garden of the Palace: if not exactly stately, it was small and elegant and took the form of a garden-pavilion, on the top of the mound, the creation of which initially caused such a commotion.

So delighted was Queen Victoria with her new summer house that she commanded Ludwig Grüner (who was to design the Mausoleum for the Prince Consort) to write and have illustrated a lavish book about it. Now extremely rare, a copy of this book, which was published in 1846 by Byron's publisher, John Murray, is to be found in the British Museum library. Bound in scarlet and gold, it is entitled *Her Majesty's Pavilion in Buckingham Palace Gardens*. The book describes the new little building as 'picturesque and fantastic, without any style of architecture'. Inside there were four rooms, one of which had facilities for cooking. The Pavilion was approached by steps and a balustraded terrace, decorated with pots of geraniums. Inside, the main room was decorated in fresco, and the classically-minded Mrs Jamison reminded readers of Grüner's book that 'the walls of garden pavilions in Italy were often decorated by the greatest artists — such as the Galatea by Raphael at the Villa Farnesina'.

The subject chosen for the decoration of the Queen's Pavilion was the *Masque of Comus*, a pastoral entertainment devised by Milton in 1634 for Lord Bridgewater, then Lord President of Wales. It was first performed in the garden of Ludlow Castle. Comus, as the erudite will remember, came of remarkable parentage: his father was Bacchus and his mother Circe. From one he inherited a tendency to get drunk; from the other an ability to cast spells — an interesting combination. The story of Comus, scenes of which were to decorate the lunette panels of the Garden Pavilion, runs, very briefly, thus: Comus waylays a maiden in a forest near Ludlow and entices her to drink a magic potion which will change her head into that of an animal. Her brothers go to her aid, and find her bound in a chair with 'chains of stone'. Unlike Comus's other captives, who now all have beasts' heads, she has so far withstood

Comus's enticements. But her brothers are unable to release her as, to do this, they must get possession of Comus's magic wand. A good spirit appears, and calls 'Sabrina fair', goddess of the nearby Severn river, for aid. Sabrina frees the captive. Comus and his beast-headed victims (one a bare-breasted maiden with a calf's head) disappear, and the rescued girl is escorted back to Ludlow Castle. Such was the story, an odd enough choice, scenes of which were to decorate the Queen's new summer house.

Of the rooms on either side of the central chamber, one was decorated with scenes from the novels of Sir Walter Scott, drawn by Grüner himself, and the other was in the Pompeiian style. Mrs Jamison, in her introduction to Grüner's book, upholds the choice of Comus as a suitable theme '. . . at once classical, romantic and pastoral . . . just the thing to inspire English artists . . . to render their task at once a light and a proud one'. And she went on '. . . nothing could be more beautifully adapted to the shades of a trim garden devoted to the recreation of our Lady Sovereign, than the chaste, polished, yet picturesque elegance of the poem'. The reason that scenes from Scott, and in the Pompeiian style, where chosen to complete the trilogy, was so that 'within a small compass, three different styles of decoration, the Cinquecento, the Antique and the Romantic might be placed in proximity and . . . brought into immediate comparison'.

Eight distinguished Royal Academicians (one for each wall of the octagonal room) were invited to co-operate in the execution of the frescos. The group was headed by Edwin Landseer, and among the others were the highlander Daniel Maclise, the marine painter Clarkson, William Etty, famous for his voluptuous female nudes, the American Charles Leslie, and Sir Charles Eastlake, a personal friend of the Queen and Prince Albert and a well-known historical painter of the time.

In her introduction, Mrs Jamison writes with great good sense: 'The application of fresco painting, in the decoration of architecture, demands the adaptation of parts to the whole . . .' and later she urges 'a harmonious combination of many minds – working under the direction of one mind, to one purpose'.

Unfortunately Mrs Jamison's recommendation was not followed. 'The eight Academicians employed on the job', writes John Steegman, 'displayed collectively that lack of

67

imaginative invention of which so many critics complained at Academy exhibitions . . . Out of the eight lunettes, three repeated one subject and two another'. Prince Albert – who though full of ideas and initiative, was only twenty-three at the time – could not 'overcome the artist's insistence each on his own arbitrary choice'. However, if the result was not totally satisfactory, the idea of having such a delightfully frivolous addition to the garden smacks of more of the eighteenth century than of the nineteenth, more of the Cinquecento than of Queen Victoria.

The 'little Casino', as the *Quarterly Review* described it, may have afforded great satisfaction to the aesthetic Albert, but the young Queen seems to have taken it very much for granted, and she does not mention it in her voluminous correspondence with her Uncle Leopold, King of the Belgians. Prince Albert recorded the progress of the work on 4th July 1845 and wrote that 'the cottage in the garden is ready, and is allowed to be seen'. *

Some space has been given to the story of the Garden Pavilion, as it has such an unexpected quality. After Prince Albert's brief entry in his diary the pavilion disappears from our narrative. Throughout the Queen's long reign, it was

A less idealized view of the Pavilion 'Picturesque and fantastic, without any style of architecture', which appeared in the *Illustrated London News* in May, 1844.
See also page 65.

*R.A. Y204/119

doubtless the scene of tea parties and children's picnics. Perhaps the Queen in her widowed years worked in it when the weather was warm, as she did in her tent in the gardens of Balmoral. One wonders if her tired eyes were ever raised from Cabinet minutes and Red Boxes, to look at the scenes of Comus's revels. Nothing, possibly, could have been more irrelevant. However, had there been room for fancy in that dedicated Royal mind, she might have seen a likeness between herself, chained to the desk (as she often described it) by her unending duties, and Comus's spellbound maiden, bound to her chair by magic links of stone. It is most unlikely: only Disraeli could have drawn her attention to it. Though, perhaps, as the Queen paused in the perusal of some particularly fatiguing memorandum, she may have looked round the exotic room, its garish colours a little faded, and remembered (if she had ever for a moment forgotten) the long gone days when she and Albert were young, beautiful and happy – and were planning a pavilion for their garden.

In 1928 the story ends. During the First World War the little building had fallen into disrepair, the frescoes had gone, and it was almost derelict. It was decided, with some regret, one hopes, to pull it down. There exists a succinct memo in Queen Mary's hand, in answer to the suggestion to this effect.

'Yes. Demolition this year, and consider a plan for another year. As we never go up there, some planting of shrubs will be quite sufficient.' *

---

*R.A. G.V. PP 18604

XIII

Garden Parties

Garden Parties (then called Breakfasts, though they took place in the afternoon) were instituted early in the reign of the young Queen Victoria. 'Breakfasts' were a popular form of entertaining in the first part of the last century and they feature in several of the Trollope political novels. Queen Victoria's Breakfasts were far smaller affairs than the modern Royal Garden Parties, and the guests at them were drawn from the inner circles of London and official society. With the death of the Prince Consort all such Royal entertainments stopped abruptly, and it was not until six years afterwards that the widowed Queen was persuaded to resume her Breakfasts. She found them 'alarming'* and Lady Longford describes the Queen's dismay at having to recognize so many people. After some years of seclusion 'it was', she found, 'all very puzzling and bewildering'. A visit to the Zoo was far less exacting.

In the 80's of the last century. Queen Victoria on the arm of her son, the Prince of Wales. Potted palms seem to have been used to add to the floral decorations.

*Victoria R.I. by Elizabeth Longford: Weidenfeld & Nicolson 1964

The Prince of Wales (afterwards Edward VII) took over much of the entertaining which was expected of the Royal Family and occasionally gave splendid garden parties in the grounds of Marlborough House. Much later in her reign the Queen was induced to attend these: and in a contemporary illustration (opposite) of the *Illustrated London News*, she is shown walking on the Prince of Wales's arm through the fashionable throng. What is interesting about the picture is the obvious lack of interest that was taken, in the eighties of the last century, in actually growing flowers in even the grandest of London gardens. The show of flowers in the Marlborough House garden appears to have had to be enhanced with the addition of some potted palms.

Garden parties – no longer called Breakfasts – were revived on a far more important scale by King George and Queen Mary. In his most interesting book *The Court of St James,** E. S. Turner writes:

> In further recognition of social changes, the King developed the garden parties which his grandmother had initiated. These were designed to admit thousands, when 'Courts' could receive only hundreds. An invitation to a garden party did not count as a presentation at Court, but it was a widely sought honour.
>
> Few citizens had suspected that Buckingham Palace could boast an attractive rear elevation, and such extensive and attractive gardens. The procedure was for the Royal Family to circulate without excessive formality among the guests, and then retire into a Durbar tent [the famous Shamiana] for special presentations. A rained-out Garden Party provided cruel amusement for the Press, for it was impossible to admit thousands of dripping guests into the Palace.

Today the garden parties are an established form of Royal entertainment. As already recorded, in an average summer three garden parties are held, and to each about nine thousand guests are invited. And there are other functions, each involving hundreds, if not thousands of people, which could only take place in the garden. Thus, the garden of the Palace

(*overleaf*) A group of elegant ladies and gentlemen on the terrace of the Pavilion at one of Her Majesty's breakfasts in the 1860s. *Illustrated London News.*

*The Court of St James, by E. S. Turner: Michael Joseph 1959

An early and uncharacteristic drawing by Sir William Russell Flint (1880–1969) of an Edwardian garden party to celebrate the engagement of Princess Margaret of Connaught to the Crown Prince of Sweden.

plays an important part in making it possible for the Sovereign to entertain large numbers of her subjects. And the lawn, laid out one hundred and fifty years ago for that much denigrated monarch, King George IV, plays an all important role.

Neither Queen Alexandra nor Queen Mary seems to have taken a great interest in the Palace garden. Queen Alexandra was not famous for her taste, except in clothes, and she belonged to a generation which took such things as gardens, especially in London, whether Palace gardens or not, very much for granted. We know she loved violets, and was seldom seen without a bunch of Parma violets in her hand, or pinned to her dress. She instituted Queen Alexandra Rose Day, inspired, it is said, by the story she had heard in her girlhood in Denmark about a poor pastor who sold the roses from his garden to help the poor of his parish.

Queen Mary was interested in antique furniture and porcelain, but not particularly in pictures and she did not, it seems, take more than a conventional interest in gardens. But she had one strong feeling, which might be called horticultural: she hated ivy.

Accustomed all her married life to trim beds of geraniums, manicured rose gardens and weedless banks of pastel-coloured hydrangeas, Queen Mary 'disliked untidiness in any form, even in plants which grew in a dishevelled manner and harboured dirt and dust: for this reason she was an inveterate and implacable foe to ivy, advising always that it should be cut down, and pulling it off walls herself, and making others do so.'

Sir Osbert Sitwell in his book *Queen Mary and Others** describes a conversation he had just before the war with King George VI, during which the King described how he and the present Queen, then a little girl, had developed ivy-poisoning from being made by Queen Mary to pull off ivy from the walls at Sandringham.

There is very little ivy in the garden at Buckingham Palace, and its absence may be explained by Queen Mary's deep antipathy to it.

(*overleaf*) The Palace from the north-west. In the foreground, Floribunda Rose, Elizabeth of Glamis, with salmon pink flowers.

Queen Mary and Others by Osbert Sitwell: Michael Joseph 1974

Part II
The Garden Today

XIV

The Terrace and Lawn

The first general view of the garden at Buckingham Palace is obtained as the visitor steps out on to the long terrace through the French windows of the ground floor. The terrace, which runs to left and right for a full one hundred and fifty yards, lies under the Nash's west façade of the Palace, and from it practically all of the garden can be seen.

But as the west façade is the garden front of the Palace, it is worth while to pause for a moment, and examine it in detail. The structure of bland Bath stone is Nash's happiest contribution to the architecture of the Palace. It was completed for George IV in the late 1820s, and was the creation of two different architects, Nash, of course, and the often belittled Edward Blore. He later was to perpetrate the dreary east façade, overlooking the Mall, which depressed Londoners from the year 1847 to 1911 ; and was only, tactfully, masked by Sir Aston Webb soon after George V's accession.

Blore's additions to Nash's west façade were, however, a definite improvement. 'Up to the line of the balustrade', writes H. Clifford Smith, 'it is as Nash left it. Above that, his four towers and central dome were removed, and the present attics were added by Blore. The effect of the addition has been to give a dignity and emphasis previously lacking to the central block.'

Nash's central dome was certainly too small and insignificant to be able to act as centrepoint to the very long west front of the Palace. As it is, the whole architectural complex is admirable – in fact, it is one of the most pleasing examples of Neo-classical building in England. In the words of that great authority Professor Sir Albert Richardson, 'It has a simple yet regal grandeur, and the level lines of the façade emphasise the projecting curves of the Central Bow. Touches here and there – for instance – the ellipsoids with ornamental surrounds, beneath the projecting portions of the cornice – recall the elegances of the Louis XVI style, and pay a compliment to Sir William Chambers.'

An apposite feature of the garden façade is Nash's elegant frieze of unglazed terra-cotta, in the form of a continuous garland of rose, thistle and shamrock. Less apposite to a garden façade are the two panels, one on either side of the Central Bow. These depict 'King Alfred expelling the Danes' and 'King Alfred delivering the Laws', and they are made of Coade Stone, a material much used at the beginning of the last century for garden sculpture and decoration. Thanks to Coade Stone's admirable qualities, these twin panels are in a state of perfect preservation and have taken on a silvery weathered appearance which blends perfectly with their setting.

A stone finial, a relic of Blore's east façade of the Palace (below left) in a setting of shrubs and daffodils.

79

An urn, signed as the work of Croggan of Lambeth, who often worked in Coade stone. The more elaborate urn beyond is slightly later in date (1835) and was the work of J. M. Blackfield. Only the Croggan urns are shown in the picture of the Palace on pages 12 and 13.

OPPOSITE
Spring blossom.

There are some fine specimens in the Royal Garden of *Pieris forrestii*, with red panaches of leaves in spring, followed by Lily-of-the-valley-like flowers.

Coade Stone is worthy, in any book dealing with gardens great or small, of a special word. It is an artificial stone, invented in about 1770 by Mrs Eleanor Coade according to a secret formula, and was manufactured by Mrs Coade's family for half a century. The secret of making this invaluable material was lost when the Coade family went out of business, and has never been rediscovered. A famous London example of Coade stone, and its extraordinary durable qualities, is to be seen in the South Bank Lion – now sited near County Hall. This noble sculpture, once a striking feature of the Hawes Brewery on the South Bank, was in danger of being lost to London when the brewery was demolished to make way for the clearing of

the South Bank site for the Festival of Britain in 1952. It is said that it was at the suggestion of King George VI that the lion was saved, and finally placed in its present commanding position.

The balustrade of the West Terrace of Buckingham Palace is also made of Coade Stone, and for its whole length is decorated, very much in the taste of the first quarter of the last century, with classical urns of the popular inverted bell shape. Nash, in his report in 1828, states that four of these vases were already in position that year. These are almost certainly the urns, with particularly delicately moulded reliefs, which were made by Croggan of Lambeth who often worked in Coade Stone. The other vases on the terrace are later in date (1835) and were made by J. M. Blackfield of Stamford. They are more elaborate than the Croggan urns, but of less finished workmanship.

Before we step down the few steps which divide the terrace of the Palace from the garden, it might be interesting to record some of the names of the head gardeners at Buckingham Palace. A list of these has been kept since early in the last century.

OPPOSITE
Tulips 'planted in a broad swathe' bring colour to the herbaceous border early in the summer.

Wyness	from 1840	
Humphrey	from 1874	(he succeeded Wyness)
Brown	1895	
Stirling	to 1901	(when the Ministry of Works took over the administration of the garden)
Courroux	1901	(for a very short time)
Osborne	1901–02	
Cole	1928	
Nutbeam	from 1954	

Two names are worthy of note. First and foremost the

admirable Mr Fred Nutbeam who will feature on several pages of this book and to whom the garden, today, owes such a debt. If there is anything in a name, surely Mr Nutbeam's symbolizes two great qualities in a gardener – toughness and cheerfulness.

The name Courroux, on the other hand, gives one to think; was he French? Courroux is a French word, though an archaic one. It occurs frequently in Racine. On engaging a gardener, good temper is a quality to be looked for. To take on, as head gardener, a Mr Rage or a Mr Anger would seem to be courting trouble. For that is what the word courroux means, and perhaps that was why he was in charge of the Royal Garden for only a few months.

From the lowest step of the terrace of the Palace to the edge of the lake, stretches the lawn which must be one of the largest and best kept in the country – and also one of the hardest worked.

The English lawn is a national tradition: elsewhere the writer has recorded that the English lawn 'is one of the few things that the British are not tiresomely modest about'. But though the word *lawn* has a very definite meaning for us in the 20th century – an area of closely mown grass – two hundred years ago, it had no such exact connotation. In fact a lawn, in the modern sense, hardly existed. When Shakespeare spoke of the 'lawnd' which Adonis, to escape from Venus, ran 'through apace', leaving 'Love upon her back, deeply distressed', he surely meant a grassy glade in a forest, rather than a smooth stretch of turf. And when Lord Tennyson preceded his two triumphantly onomatopeic lines

> The moan of doves in immemorial elms
> And murmuring of innumerable bees

with the words

> Myriads of rivulets hurrying through the lawn

he probably had in mind a grassy field.

It so happened, however, that when the future Poet Laureate was twenty-two, a young man with the far less distinguished name of Budding, invented a machine which was to give the word lawn the meaning it has had ever since. Geoffrey Taylor, in his richly informative book *Some Nineteenth-Century Gardeners* writes with sympathy of Edwin Budding '. . . the inventor of the lawn mower, as never achieving fame' as did the inventor of the safety razor. You may seek in vain for the name of Budding in the *Dictionary of National Biography* . . . who, in 1836, patented a 'machine for cropping or shearing the vegetable surface of lawns, grass-plots etc.' *

Before Edwin Budding's revolutionary invention, lawns had to be cut by scythe, and when Queen Charlotte lived in the Queen's House, this was certainly the method employed. And to scythe a lawn successfully, grass has to be wet, so scything had to be done soon after dawn. That was how the famous *Tapis vert*, pride of the garden of Versailles, was kept in trim. But even with an army of gardeners at work, the Kings of France in all probability never knew such smooth and faultless turf as is now taken for granted in any suburban villa. And that is thanks to the inventive mind of the unsung Mr Budding.

The view that greets visitors to the Queen's garden, as they stand at the top of the terrace steps, might be the prospect enjoyed from the garden terrace of a large country house in the depths of the country: or rather such was the view until the recent development of the Stag Brewery site between Buckingham Palace Road and Victoria. Now, instead of an

An illustration of Edwin Budding's invention the lawn mower, from *The Gardener's Magazine*, 1832.

Some Nineteenth-Century Gardeners by Geoffrey Taylor: Skeffington 1951

unbroken horizon of trees, a towering new block of flats and offices rears its unlovely head above the trees: and from its upper stories the Palace Garden can be overlooked. Its privacy has been destroyed. To counter this, and to enable the occupants of the Palace to walk round the garden unobserved by human eye or telescopic lens, a short avenue of Indian chestnuts (*Aesculus indica*) has been planted below the terrace steps. This leads, diagonally, across the lawn, to the shelter and privacy of lofty trees, and thickly planted shrub-borders.

Beyond the lawn lies the lake, with its island and promontories. Both lake and lawn are set in a rich framework of trees. To the north and west the skyline is, as yet, more or less unbroken by high rise building.

The lawn of the garden at Buckingham Palace is as fair an example of a perfectly kept stretch of turf as could be found in the whole country; it must be one of the largest and most beautiful lawns in the world. The crucial test of well kept turf is its powers of recuperation. When I was starting my research on the Royal garden, it was in late July, at the height of the great drought of 1976. From the Palace steps to the border of the lake, the lawn stretched as brown and dusty, it must be said, as an old door mat. Over and above this, it had just undergone the tramping of fifty-four thousand feet – two (presumably) for each of Her Majesty's twenty-seven thousand guests at the three annual Garden Parties. Workmen, in jeans and little else, were dismantling the requisite tents – poles, bits of wood, and canvas lay about. There was a strict ban on watering, as rigorously observed in the Palace garden as in the garden of any semi-detached villa in the suburbs. As a result, the Royal lawn looked a mess.

Soon after, it rained: and in September, on my second visit, the scene had changed completely. All was green once more, and it was as if the drought had never been: which speaks highly for the good condition of the Royal lawn, the efficiency of the garden staff, and the recuperative powers of well prepared British turf.

As the lawn in the Royal garden covers much the largest single part of it, it might be of interest to record the composition of grasses which make up such a famous stretch of turf. Most of the lawn is of Bent grasses, but Smooth-Stalked Meadow grass is included, as are Rye grass and Dog's Tail grass. The shaded areas under the trees are planted with annual meadow grass. The soil of the turf is regularly fertilized, and the lawn is kept as weed free as possible. But there are, of course, some daisies and yarrow, and 'bright green patches of camomile are encouraged to spread'. There has never been, as such, a camomile lawn at Buckingham Palace, though this has often been written about. But camomile, *Anthemis nobilis*, certainly makes an integral part of the Royal turf and is, by hand planting, occasionally increased.

There is another story about the camomile in the lawn at Buckingham Palace; and a statement has often been made that, not only is a great part of the lawn entirely composed of camomile, but of a very special non-flowering variety, an obvious advantage in any plant used for lawn-making. After some research, I succeeded in tracing the source of this rumour, for rumour, only, it is. It seems that some years ago a guest at a Royal Garden Party – a keen gardener – examined the famous lawn with expert interest, saw some camomile growing in the grass, and could not resist taking up a bit, roots and all. This, she (it is said that it was a she) duly planted in her own garden, where it thrived; and proved to be a kind of camomile which is flowerless. Hence the story spread that the whole of the Buckingham Palace lawn was formed of 'non-flowering camomile'. Mr Nutbeam and his colleagues must sometimes wish that it was so, but it is not.

A camomile said to be non-flowering and perhaps a descendant of the original stray, is marketed under the name of *Anthemis nobilis* Treneague. Incidentally, a flowerless anthemis is something of a contradiction in terms, as the plant's very name, anthemis, derives from the Greek *anthemon*, a flower, 'in reference to their . . . floriferous character' (*R.H.S. Dictionary*).

Camomile is a native plant to London, and to the district of Westminster in particular. Earlier in this book mention of *Chamaemelum nobilis* was recorded by William Camden in his 16th-century book *Britannia – or a Chorographical Description of Great Britain and Ireland* as growing in 'Tuttle-fields' near the Abbey.

All camomiles, flowerless or not, seem to be plants with masochistic tendencies. They thrive on ill-treatment. Falstaff in *Henry IV (Part I)* says 'The more it is trodden on the faster it

Camomile (*Anthemis nobilis* or *Chamaemelum*) from Gerard's *Herball*, published in 1597.

grows', adding with a sigh 'yet youth, the more it is wasted, the sooner it wears'.

Later in this book examples of unexpected wild life to be found in the Royal garden will be described in detail. But it must be borne in mind that though the garden, for most of the year, is secluded – and so is often described as an oasis in the middle of a great city – it is still an oasis which is invaded three or four times a year by thousands of garden-party guests and, far worse, and for weeks at a time, by the small army of caterers, contractors and workmen who put up the necessary tents; the last, especially, being no respecters of the shelter and occasional convenience provided by shrubs and bushy undergrowth round the lake: and they have little regard for the privacy of *Nyroca ferina* (pochard) or *Dictyna viridissima*, (an unusual green spider), which might want to make their nests or webs there.

'. . . examined the famous lawn with expert interest, saw some camomile growing there . . . and could not resist taking up a bit, roots and all'. Drawing by Hugh Robson.

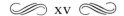 XV

The Lake

A great charm of the lake in the Royal garden is the way in which the borders have been left in an almost natural state. The vegetation by the water's edge is thick and lush, ideal cover, apart from occasional disturbance, for ducks and water-side creatures. Most of the plants, some of which over the years have grown into impressive clumps, are indigenous to England. The Common Reedmace, *Typha latifolia*, and the Bulrush, *Scirpus lacustris*, abound, as does Sagittaria, with its arrow-shaped leaves, as well as other ordinary water-side plants, amongst them *Arundo donax* and *Phragmites communis*, Yarrow (Achillea) and Ox-eye Daisies (*Telekia speciosa*). Here and there occurs the noble *Osmunda regalis*, which has been mentioned earlier, as having 'once upon a time' provided shelter for an early British princess from the invading Danes. The Osmunda by the Buckingham Palace lake must certainly have been planted, as when the lake was first dug it was already an unusual plant to be found growing in the wild. Two other plants which delight in the moist soil bordering the lake are the Lesser Knotweed (*Polygonum compactum*) and the very similar Japanese Knotweed (*P. cuspidatum*) which grows very strongly, and of which the rhizomes are apt to invade the nearby lawn and flower beds. This is a plant with bronze-coloured stems, highly decorative in winter, and worth leaving uncut for its pictorial value.

Another plant which grows by the lakeside is definitely an exotic – the giant *Gunnera manicata*, with its enormous spreading leaves. Gunnera originates in Brazil, though it has become acclimatized in many British gardens. But is needs winter cover, and likes to be tucked up under a covering of its own dead leaves before the first frosts.

Gunnera was a favourite waterside plant of that great gardener Miss Gertrude Jekyll, who once wrote: 'It was a good day for our water-margins when the giant gunnera were

Contrasting foliage by the lake. The spearlike leaves of *Phormium tenax* next to the finer fronds of the Royal Fern (*Osmunda regalis*).

introduced; for the immense size and noble form of their foliage enable us to make water pictures on a scale that before was impossible.'

In a garden on as large a scale as that of the Palace, gunnera look perfectly in place.

The lake gave trouble as early as 1840 when the muddy banks were reinforced with Kent flints, three-hundred tons of them. Fourteen years later there was more trouble when the water was found to be impure, and there was a suggestion, mentioned by Lord Palmerston, that the lake should be drained completely and converted into flower beds. This was not done, but elaborate arrangements were made to maintain a healthy flow of clean water. Fish were introduced, and appeared to thrive, though they had to be removed to Kensington Gardens in 1869 when the whole lake was concreted. They were afterwards returned. In the hot August of 1883 there was a serious scare when the water in the lake was reported to have been in a bad state all the summer, and on occasions the smell was offensive. This was suspected to be the result of the blocking of the inlets and the gardeners (one head gardener – ten underlings) complained about having to work by the waterside. Some years before there had been two cases of typhoid at Buckingham Palace, and the lake came under immediate suspicion, for the Prince Consort himself had died of typhoid, almost certainly caused by the bad drains at Windsor Castle. But an expert took samples of the water and declared them wholesome, even 'of excellent quality for dietetic purposes'. Gradually over the years, the water system was improved and the bed of the lake kept clean. In 1941 the job of draining and cleaning was most efficiently done by a gang of German prisoners-of-war.

There was an exchange of memos on the subject of fish for the lake, in May 1902 – soon after King Edward VII's accession to the throne. *

These passed between the Earl of Denbigh, a Lord in Waiting, and Lord Knollys, Private Secretary to the King. Lord Denbigh suggested that the lake should be stocked with Rainbow Trout, as not only would this be an interesting experiment from the fish culturists' point of view, but if 'a little trouble were taken about it, it is quite possible that they might thrive . . . and provide some sport for the Prince of Wales, and other fishermen'. But, Lord Denbigh pointed out, Rainbow Trout had to feed, and besides the fish themselves, he offered 'snails, fresh water shrimps and other things that fish eat'. Furthermore he suggested that water lilies, reeds and bulrushes should be planted, as these would add very favourably to the appearance of the lake. He offered to send to London, from his fishery in North Wales, six baskets of growing bulrushes: but as these baskets were heavy, he suggested telephoning to the Equerry, to ask 'if some luggage

*Ed. VII Personal Papers A.9458

conveyance could meet the 11.10 at Euston . . . to take the baskets'.

Knowing what damage water fowl can do to young plantations, Lord Denbigh further proposed that the swans and ducks on the Buckingham Palace lake should be temporarily banished to the water in St James's Park, to remain there until the bulrushes were established.

At that time the bird population of the lake, according to a contemporary note, consisted of fifty ducks, four black swans and two geese.

King Edward approved this elaborate operation on May 6th. There is no record of the ultimate fate of the Rainbow Trout, but the bulrushes prospered and, at one time, almost entirely surrounded the borders of the lake.

The exact area of the lake was unknown for a long time. Owing to its irregular outline, it was difficult to measure accurately, until an ingenious solution to the problem was devised.

Dr Bristowe, one of the distinguished group of experts who carried out a survey of the garden in 1964, as will be described in detail later, tells how the exact measurements ($3\frac{3}{4}$ acres) of the lake were arrived at. In a BBC broadcast about the garden at Buckingham Palace, having modestly affirmed that he was not the clever man who solved the problem, he went on to say '. . . I was thrilled how it was done, because it was so simple. They had a map of the garden, and they cut it out very carefully with scissors, and weighed the paper on which the map was drawn on a very sensitive balance. Having done that, they took up the scissors again, and cut out the very irregular lake. And then they deducted the weight of the paper on which the lake was printed, from the weight of the map, and got the area that way.'

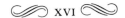
The Trees

The garden at Buckingham Palace is planted with many fine trees, and some of these are not the usual trees that one would expect to find in a garden, however large, in the middle of a great city. True, there are plane trees a-plenty – those workaday, but infinitely valuable trees for any planting in a big town – for plane trees, and most especially the London plane (*Platanus acerifolia*) are particularly well adapted to thrive under town conditions; they have been planted in the streets of London since the early 18th century and in London they are planted in greater numbers than all the other sorts of trees put together; for the plane has the faculty of standing up better than any other known tree to city conditions, to extremes of heat and damp, to indifferent soil, and to polluted air. For a long time this particular ability was ascribed to the habit of the plane tree of shedding its bark, and that great authority, W. J. Bean, records 'this theory has been religiously repeated by nearly every writer ever since', but he goes on to

'The Plane has the faculty of standing up better than other known tree to city conditions.'

The west façade of the Palace under a canopy of trees. The garden covers an area of about 39 acres.

say, that 'there is no proof of this, for atmospheric influences do not affect branches large enough to shed their bark, but rather the leaves, and other breathing parts of the tree'. The genus platanus originates on the dry, sunburnt slopes of Greece and Asia Minor. It is strange, but extremely fortunate, that it should have been able to make itself so at home in the very different climate of so many northern European cities.

As well as plane trees, there are, in the Royal garden, many of the stalwart trees and shrubs relied on by every sensible city gardener, such as the spotted laurel (*Aucuba japonica*), silver birches (*Betulus pendula*), beeches (*Fagus sylvatica*), different hollies (*ilex*) and several clumps of that much underrated shrub for use in town gardens – the golden privet. All these are everyday sort of plant material, but how poor and unfurnished any town garden of any size would look without them. In the garden of Buckingham Palace they make a background and provide shelter for the more interesting trees and shrubs which

The new avenue of Indian Chestnuts (*Aesculus indica*) in flower. There are 2½ miles of gravel paths all uniformly wide, to take cars and lorries and, in the past, Queen Victoria's pony and trap.

have been planted in the garden, especially in the last forty years.

One of the most interesting trees in the Royal garden is a tall and impressive *Taxodium distichum* – the swamp or deciduous cypress. This is to be found in the neighbourhood of the Waterloo Vase (see facing page 64), and its lofty conical outline is clearly to be seen, especially in winter when the surrounding trees are bare, by observant passengers on the top of a bus going up or down Grosvenor Place.

The swamp cypress was introduced into this country from Louisiana in the early 17th century, and the London herbalist John Parkinson, in his *Theatrum Botanicum* (published in 1640) praises it highly, though he suggests that it is not a 'true Cipresse' but might have got its name from the cypress-like fragrance of its wood. Parkinson tells us that the first seed of taxodium was brought to England from America by 'Master Tradescant' (gardener to James I) and, once the seed was sown, that it 'sprang, verie bravelie'. Baron von Humboldt records that there were taxodiums in another Royal garden nearly five hundred years ago, when there were fine specimens in the Palace garden at Chapultepec; and John Loudon quotes Sir Henry Ward, who was Minister in Mexico in the last century, as mentioning a 'Cypress of Montezuma . . . which had attained its full height when that unfortunate monarch was on the throne of Mexico in 1520', so that when Ward saw it, it must have been at least four hundred years old.

The swamp cypress in the Buckingham Palace garden is a fine tree, though it can not be more than one hundred and fifty years old. It was probably planted when Aiton was reorganizing the garden, and landscaping it for George IV.

Taxodiums are interesting for one particular reason. They delight in being planted near, or actually in water: when set in swampy ground they produce an extraordinary form of root-growth, which is said to be unique in nature: this is a kind of upright woody protuberance, called a 'knee' – or more technically, a pneumatophore. These knees, which are sometimes ten to fifteen inches high, are smooth, hollow and knobbly. They are now known to be an integral part of the breathing system of the submerged roots, but two hundred years ago they very much perplexed the celebrated French botanist André Michaux (1746–1803), when he first saw them.

'No cause', he wrote, 'can be assigned for their existence: they are peculiar to the deciduous cypress . . . they are made use of by negroes as beehives.'

There are some magnificent taxodiums – complete with 'knees', in the park at Syon.

Two other fine trees in the Royal garden are *Sophora japonica* and a particularly effective *Acer saccharinum*.

Sophora japonica which, incidentally, is not a native of Japan but of China was named by Linnaeus from the Arabian name for a tree with pea-like flowers, sophera. Like taxodium it is deciduous, and it is described by W. J. Bean as 'one of the most beautiful of all leguminous trees in England'. But it bears its flowers uncomfortably late in the season, sometimes not until September, and after very cold summers it refuses to flower at all. But after a warm dry July and August it can be completely covered with white, butterfly-shaped flowers (which the *R.H.S. Dictionary*, in its enthusiasm, describes as 'papilionaceous'), and it presents a truly exquisite sight. Its flowers do not fade on the tree, but fall while quite fresh, whitening the ground beneath.

The silver maple (*Acer saccharinum*) has been growing in English gardens since 1725, and is one of the loveliest of all maples – especially when the wind ruffles the silver undersides of the leaves on its slender pendant branches. It is a tree of graceful habit, a native of North America, and its foliage puts up a bright show of red and yellow in autumn.

Long lists of Latin names can make tedious reading. But a few of the more unusual trees to be found growing in the garden, which are worthy of mention, would include several specimens of two other rather special maples. *Acer palmatum* Atropurpureum, with its wine-dark leaves, and *Acer palmatum* Senkaki (in Japanese, Sangokaku), the coral bark maple, a particularly valuable tree in winter as its younger branches are coloured coral red.

Ailanthus altissima is not a great rarity, but its picturesque outline always attracts attention. Known as the Tree of Heaven – in its native China it grows so tall that its branches are said to touch the sky – ailanthus in England is a tree of more modest proportions. Some ingenious gardeners, with an eye for the effect of fine foliage, cut young trees of ailanthus down to the ground each spring as they might *Cornus sibirica*. Treated in this way, the Tree of Heaven forgets its celestial aspirations, and puts forth enormous leaves, each 3–4 feet in length, and at a little higher than eye-level.

A buddleia which grows well in the Royal garden is one which is usually only found in the gardens of connoisseurs – *Buddleia alternifolia*. This is one of the best of the butterfly bushes, and is at its most effective if allowed to grow free standing; unlike its *B. davidii* relations, it should be given the lightest of pruning after flowering.

A few other trees are worth special mention; a tulip tree, *Liriodendron tulipifera*, one of the most beautiful trees in the world, was planted in 1956 in the Palace garden, and is making good progress. A young tree does not produce the curious tulip-shaped flowers which are so distinctive, but the oddly shaped leaves which turn a bright guinea gold in the autumn make liriodendron a tree worth having in any garden. It was introduced into England from North America in 1688 – the year of the so-called Glorious Revolution, which saw the replacement on the throne of James II, the father of 'Princess Buckingham', by William III.

Three other trees which display the very special taste and imagination with which the garden has been planted under the direction of King George VI, Queen Elizabeth and the present Queen in the last thirty or forty years, are *Paulownia tomentosa* (or *imperialis*) with blue, hyacinth-shaped bracts of flowers in early spring. These are all too often caught by a late frost. Paulownia gets its name from a botanizing Grand Duchess of Russia, Anna Paulovna, younger sister of the Grand Duchess Catherine, who took such an instantaneous dislike to George IV when Prince Regent: she afterwards became Queen of Holland. *Photinia beauvardiana*, a small Chinese tree of great charm with flowers like hawthorn and bright autumn fruit and colour; and a medium-sized tree which would give distinction to any arboretum in the country and which seems to have settled down happily in the middle of London, *Nyssa sylvatica* – the Tupelo from the Eastern United States and Mexico, where it loves to grow by water (Nyssa was a Greek water-nymph). It is of columnar habit and it, too, turns a rich scarlet in autumn. Like many trees which, in their native, warmer climates, like to grow with their roots in water, nyssa in chillier latitudes prefers a drier site in rich, not too saturated loam.

The contorted form of this Sweet Chestnut (*Castanea sativa*) by the lake suggests that it was once a Japanese Bonsai.

Another tree in the Royal garden deserves a special word. Not rare in itself – it is an ordinary sweet chestnut – it is quite extraordinary in its form. This curiously contorted tree would surely have a special history to recount if, like the Oaks of Dodona, it had the gift of speech. It resembles a giant bonsai, if it is not too much a contradiction in terms to describe a dwarf tree as a giant. One wonders if it was a gift from some Japanese ambassador to Queen Alexandra and if, perhaps, its first

Rhododendrons flourish in beds laced with peat.

Buckingham Palace must be one of the few Royal gardens in the world not to have any fountains – but there is a cascade, to give coolness and the sound of running water.

novelty having passed, the Queen suggested it should be planted in the garden. Whatever its story, there it is today, twenty feet high, but still retaining its original twisted shape.

Before leaving the subject of the larger trees in the Royal garden, note must be made of one which always attracts attention and interest. This is the mulberry – growing in the south-west corner of the garden, near the greenhouses and the Head Gardener's house. It is labelled as one of the original mulberries planted on James I's instructions in the early 17th century, as we have described on earlier pages of this book. If

OPPOSITE
The Admiralty Summer House in the rose garden (*see page 126*).

The Head Gardener's house might be in the depths of the country.

the story is true that King James's project of planting mulberries to encourage the silkworm industry failed because he was wrongly advised in the type of mulberry to plant, the supposedly surviving mulberry would corroborate the theory. It is a *Morus nigra* (which silkworms do not like to feed on), and not a *Morus alba* (which they do). But it is certainly not more than two hundred years old, and therefore could not possibly be part of the original planting.

These, therefore, are just a few of the trees which grow in the garden of Buckingham Palace. But it must be borne in mind that, with every season, there are losses as well as additions. The Palace garden, like all good gardens, is a living, changing thing. Its collection of plants and trees never remains static. Under the enterprising direction of Mr Nutbeam, the best new varieties of plants are continually being added to replace trees that are past their prime, encroach on new young plantations, or quite simply take up too much space. For even in a Royal garden of forty acres, space is not unlimited.

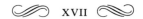
Camellias, Magnolias and other Shrubs

Since 1954 – when Mr Nutbeam became head gardener at Buckingham Palace – an impressive collection of camellias has been assembled.

Camellias are some of the most beautiful and practical shrubs for town gardeners – whether their garden is half the size of a tennis court, or of Royal dimensions. They are first mentioned as a plant grown in English gardens in John Ray's *Historia Plantarum*, published in 1704. Most camellias originate in the Orient, though there are some that are natives of North America.

Camellias get their mellifluous name, like so many other plants, from Linnaeus, who named them after Georg Kamel, a simple Jesuit priest, a native of Moravia, who travelled to the Philippines and collected seeds of the plants which he found there. Some years after his death his good work for botany was recognized when his name was given to a particularly beautiful variety of the tea plant, which the Chinese called *T'e* pronounced *cha* in Mandarin, a word which has a homely connotation for any British ex-serviceman.

Linnaeus, in christening his particular pink-flowered tea plant camellia latinized the Jesuit's name, Kamel, to Camellus (there being no K in the Latin alphabet) – and so the word camellia was born; a beautiful name for one of the most beautiful of trees. Oddly enough, the British, who have their own ways with pronunciation, are usually quite unable to pronounce the word camellia correctly – insisting, for some reason, on pronouncing the second syllable to rhyme with feel, instead of with fell, which is both illogical and wrong. The French get it right, perhaps owing to Alexandre Dumas' unhappy heroine, La Dame aux Camélias.

Queen Victoria, whose mentions in her letters and diaries of plants and gardens are, for any garden historian, so disappointingly rare, actually has a word for the camellia. In March 1849

Camellia sasanqua

Mr Fred Nutbeam, head gardener at the Palace since 1954. 'If there is anything in a name . . . Mr Nutbeam's symbolizes two great qualities in a gardener, toughness and cheerfulness'.

the Queen wrote to her uncle, King Leopold of the Belgians, from Osborne, saying: 'If we have no mountains to boast of, we have the sea, which is ever enjoyable: and we have CAMELLIAS which have stood out two winters covered, with RED flowers. . . . Does this not sound tempting?' *

Until recently, most people thought, as did Queen Victoria, that camellias were delicate, but they are not. If protected from the early morning sun (which they do not like, especially after frost) and planted in acid soil, camellias are among the hardiest and least demanding of shrubs.

King George VI and Queen Elizabeth were extremely fond

*Letters of Queen Victoria, vol. II

of all flowering trees and during their occupancy of Buckingham Palace, hampered by six years of war, the general quality of the planting of the garden was immensely improved. Dark and depressing evergreens were replaced – though the overall framework was retained – with magnolias, cherries and, especially, camellias. These were obviously favourite plants.

Among the collection of camellias in the Royal garden are to be found such general favourites as Adolphe Audusson, with its blood red flowers; Alba Simplex, white and single flowered; and a cross between Alba Simplex and one of the best and longest flowering of all camellias, Gloire de Nantes, the white and pink Lady Vansittart; the early flowering dark, red Althiiflora; the parti-coloured Tricolor; and two of the most elegant and exotic of all camellias, with names to match, Countess Lavinia Maggi and Princess Bacciochi. Both are called after women who were probably beauties of the French Second Empire, Princess Bacciochi almost certainly being the daughter-in-law of Elisa Bacciochi, Napoleon's sister, who played a part in the creation of the Waterloo Vase, mentioned later in this book.

The list of the camellias in the garden at Buckingham Palace is a long one, and is constantly being added to, but two more could still be singled out for special mention, Sasanqua and Saluenensis: Sasanqua because of its heartening habit of showing its small exquisite flowers so early in the year, sometimes soon after Christmas; and Saluenensis because it was first found growing on the banks of the Salween river in Burma, which was the scene of such fierce and inconclusive fighting in May 1944, twenty years after.

In another book, *Flowers in History*,* I have written: 'Camellias are sometimes criticized for dying untidily, and when their flowers are frosted, and the petals fail to fall, a camellia with its branches hung with browning flowers can look depressing: but some varieties, ''Donation'', for instance, die like aristocrats.' It must have been such a camellia which encouraged the Victorian poet Michael Field to describe the petals of a dying camellia flower as 'breaking . . . on the sudden, from their mass, and all the action stately as a funeral'.

Donation is a hybrid of Camellia Saluenensis, from the Salween river.

Azalea mollis

*Weidenfeld & Nicolson 1970

When the camellias are just past their first flush, the magnolias come into glorious flower. I have often thought how fortunate it is that magnolias – the most elegant of trees – should have received, also from Linnaeus, the most elegant of names. It was Linnaeus's practice, as is well-known, to name plants after deserving or celebrated figures in the world of botany. Magnolias received their present name in 1753, having before then been known, rather cumbrously, as laurel tulip trees: they were called after a French provincial doctor – Pierre Magnol – who was born in 1638 and died in 1715. For most of his life he directed the botanical garden at Montpellier. But it was not merely for his horticultural work that the great Linnaeus rechristened the beautiful Laurel Tulip with the worthy doctor's name. Magnol 'concut l'idée féconde du classement des plantes par famille' . . . fecund indeed, for the whole thinking structure of the Linnaean system of nomenclature of plants derives from Dr Magnol's inspiration. Once again, how lucky it is that the doctor's name should have been what it was – he might have been called Schmidt.

There is a fine collection of magnolias in the garden of Buckingham Palace, both of the Oriental varieties, and of the slightly less spectacular kinds which originate in the New World. In the East, magnolias have always been highly prized, though not only for their flowers. At one time they were grown mainly on account of their bark which, when powdered, was considered to be an effective aphrodisiac.

One of the strongest growing of oriental magnolias, well represented in the Royal garden, is M. kobus – a native of Japan, and much used in that country as a stock plant. It is a generous flowerer, but only when well-established – a magnolia for patient gardeners; another variety from the Far East is Magnolia sieboldii (syn parviflora), which makes a small and shapely tree, and bears sweetly-scented, small flowers of which the great attraction is their bosse of rosy crimson stamens. M. sieboldii is a comparative newcomer to Western gardens, and it is recorded as having first flowered at Kew in 1893. It is named after Phillip von Siebold who introduced many fine plants from the Far East in the last century.

A third beautiful magnolia to be seen in the Royal garden is M. stellata. This is one of the best of all the smaller magnolias, and though it originates in Japan, it was introduced into

England from America in 1877. Its flowers are long-petalled and starry-shaped, and it is one of the most suitable of magnolias for the more modest gardens of today. It flowers when quite young, and seldom grows more than six feet high, though it has the welcome quality of looking picturesque and mature fairly early in life.

I remember with some amusement an incident when, a few years ago, I was on a garden tour of America. I was taken to the house of a keen amateur gardener near Philadelphia. It was March, and there was little colour: American gardens, at least in the Northern States, come into bloom later than their equivalents in England. But from the drawing room window a splendid group of *Magnolia stellata* could be seen. I admired them saying, 'How splendidly your stellatas are flowering.' 'No, Mr Coats,' came a quick reproof. 'Those are not stellas, they are Star Magnolias.'

Magnolia grandiflora, an American plant born and bred, flowers well in the Buckingham Palace garden. It was introduced into European gardens from the southern United States in the 18th century, and that great authority, W. J. Bean, calls it 'the finest flowered of evergreen trees'. It has embellished many a Georgian façade of mellow red brick for nearly three hundred years. One cannot imagine roses, wistaria or even a majestic magnolia growing on the walls of Buckingham Palace, but it so happens that *Magnolia grandiflora* is usually grown in the protection of a wall in England, though it will make an impressive free-standing tree in a fairly sheltered position. The combination of its shining leaves, bottle green on top and warm brown velvet beneath, its globe-shaped, scented flowers, and its overall air of distinction make it a noble addition to any garden.

A picture of one of the most beautiful of magnolias in the garden is shown facing page 65. This is *M. soulangeana*, called after a famous horticulturist, Etienne Soulange-Bodin, once the curator of Malmaison, where the Empress Joséphine had a world-famous garden. Among the thousands of flowers she grew there were some which had certainly reached Malmaison through the gallantry of George IV, then Prince Regent, who instructed that plants addressed to the Empress should be allowed through the British blockade of France.

One more magnolia, bred from the outstanding *M.*

soulangeana, deserves a word. This is *M. soulangeana* Picture, raised at the famous Rothschild garden at Exbury less than twenty years ago. Picture's other parent was *M. liliflora nigra*, and it too has the great advantage of flowering when quite a young tree. Its white blossoms are upstanding, and streaked with winey-purple on the outside. The tree in the Palace garden was the first specimen to be sent out from its parent nursery.

One cultural hint about growing magnolias successfully has stood me in good stead through many years of my practical garden life. It is often forgotten that magnolias in the wild are forest or open woodland trees, and therefore they are used, in nature, to an annual mulch of dead leaves. Too often, in highly cultivated Western gardens, magnolias are grown as free-standing specimen trees on lawns, or growing out of paving on terraces, or in the narrow, dry, earth-space next to the walls of a house. Grown in this way they do not receive the yearly rich mulch of decaying vegetable matter which provides their natural nourishment. Sometimes, even when grown in shrub borders, the ground beneath them is kept so tidy that all dead leaves are carefully raked out and taken away. So mulch magnolias with a generous helping of dead leaves every autumn to retain moisture and feed their roots, and they will flower more generously than ever before, and fairly illuminate the corner of the garden in which they are planted.

Shrubs are surely the most labour-saving of all groups of plants. Their growth is restrained, their natures are easy going, they ask for very little; they are without ideas above their station. 'We are your shrubs, no cedars, we', says Titus Andronicus, modestly. And it is this general good temper and ease of culture which have earned shrubs the important part they play in English gardens today. Given the soil and situation which suits them, shrubs are extraordinarily generous in flower, in fruit, in form and in autumn colour.

As in every well-planted garden of today, there are many interesting shrubs in the garden at Buckingham Palace.

A list of just a few would certainly include *Andromeda polifolia*, a more attractive plant than the *R.H.S. Dictionary* would have us believe ('diffuse and straggly'), but the Bog Rosemary or Moonwort is one of the longest flowering plants in the garden, and its rosy pendent flowers are borne for months on end. It is the only true andromeda, though other plants sometimes pass under the same name, including cassiope, leucothoë, and two others which grow in the Royal Garden, pieris and zenobia.

Pieris is a good-looking evergreen shrub, of which the chief beauty is the new young spring leaf growth. This is far more spectacular than the flowers, though these are attractive and sweet-smelling. But it is the scarlet panaches of leaves of pieris, and especially of *Pieris forrestii*, which take the eye in spring.

In a corner of the garden near Hyde Park Corner, there is a fine clump of white Japanese tree peony, Mrs William Kelway.

Pieris likes to grow in acid soil and, unexpectedly, makes a first-class pot or tub-plant under town conditions. There are some fine specimens in the Royal garden grouped near the *Taxodium distichum*.

Another unusual shrub, which in the past has been referred to as *Andromeda dealbata*, is *Zenobia pulverulenta*. It differs from its close relation, pieris, by being almost deciduous, and produces its lily-of-the-valley-like, aniseed-scented flowers in June and July. It is a plant only found in the gardens of discerning gardeners, and the *R.H.S. Dictionary of Shrubs in Colour* praises it with the words '. . . seldom seen in gardens, and deserves to be better known for its quiet beauty'.

Caryopteris, from the Greek *karyon*, a nut, and *pteron*, a wing, from the shape of its fruit, is a sub-shrub which shows its bright blue flowers at a time of year – August – before the Michaelmas daisies have got under way when blue is a valuable colour in the garden. It is a native of Asia, and the best variety is the one grown in the Palace garden, *C. clandonensis*, which was raised at Clandon, in Surrey, about half a century ago.

Another shrub which shares caryopteris's quality of bringing blue to the shrub border in late summer, is *Ceratostigma willmottianum*, called after a great Edwardian amateur gardener, Miss Ellen Willmott, whose garden at Warley in Essex was once celebrated. Miss Willmott, a rich woman and a passionate gardener, spent her entire fortune on her garden. Such was her extravagance that in one year she is said to have planted ten thousand camassia bulbs.

I remember being taken, as a boy, to see Miss Willmott at Warley. The garden was kept perfectly, and was still full of colour. The house was extremely shabby. It was an autumn afternoon, and we were invited to stay and share her evening meal – a small jug of Bovril. Outside the front door were three newly delivered magnolias, their roots still bound up in sacking. They were almost full grown and, even in those long ago days, must have cost a fortune.

Ceratostigma is a bright blue relation of the plumbago, and *C. willmottianum* is the best variety. It worthily commemorates a great English gardener, and her unfortunate passion.

Quite a different shrub is *Cotinus coggygria*, until recently known as *Rhus cotinus*. Ceratostigma, in cold winters, sometimes dies down altogether, and behaves as if it were herbaceous. Cotinus, all the year round, presents a sturdy bush, deciduous but upstanding. Colloquially known as the Smoke Tree, cotinus is a very lovely thing in summer when in the full panoply of wine-red leaves and covered with clouds of vaporous flowers, from which it gets its name. Cotinus is a member of the Sumach family, and its bark, when professionally treated, provides a useful dye. *C. coggygria*, the variety grown in the Royal garden, is the best and most richly-coloured of the group, in spite of its ugly name.

The viburnum family is enormous, and some of the best shrubs in the garden belong to it, and one of the very best of the group is *Viburnum carlesii*, introduced to the west from Korea in the year of King Edward VII's Coronation. *V. carlesii* has every quality – a neat habit, dapper leaves of soft green and, above all, the most highly-scented flowers imaginable. It is at its best in April and May.

These, then, are some of the more interesting shrubs to be found growing in the garden at Buckingham Palace. There are many more, but the few chosen for special mention show the variety of the collection. Without being said to be pampered, all are, within reason, given the growing conditions they prefer. Calcifuges are set in built-up beds of peat, and liberally mulched. Lime-lovers have lime dug into the soil at planting time. And considering that all grow in the heart of what is still one of the largest cities in the world, with its high content of soot in the atmosphere in spite of the Clean Air Bill, all the trees and shrubs in the garden look remarkably healthy, happy and well cared for.

XVIII

The Herbaceous Border

The herbaceous border in the Royal garden is of Royal dimensions – one-hundred-and-seventy yards long and seven yards deep. But though few gardens these days have space for such imposing plantings, all the experts for the last hundred years have said that to be totally successful and to achieve their maximum effect, herbaceous borders must be on a generous scale. In recent years it has been rather fashionable to denigrate them. Their fall from favour was due, comprehensibly, to the amount of work they entail, as much as from the change of taste. But a border of hardy herbaceous plants, especially if intermingled with groups of suitable shrubs and evergreens – or, even better, ever-greys – does not need all the attention that the inexperienced gardener might think. Many herbaceous plants, once planted, and planted right, in well-prepared soil and in the correct situation, need little or no after care. Of peonies, for instance, it has been said, that they actually thrive on neglect and only ask to be left alone. And a clump of peonies can increase in beauty for thirty years.

A well-planted herbaceous border can present a dazzling picture for a quarter of the year – and if some judicious interplanting (of tulips, in season, or of annuals later) can be undertaken, as is done in the Palace border, the display can be even further prolonged.

Nearly a century ago when herbaceous borders were a new idea, that great Victorian gardener William Robinson had words of his usual wisdom to say on the subject, though the phrase herbaceous border was not so generally used then as it is now. From the high standard of excellence of the Palace border, it would seem that Mr Nutbeam has studied the Robinson precepts carefully.

General borders may be made in various ways; but it may be well to bear in mind the following points: Select only good plants; throw away weedy kinds; there is no scarcity of the best ... Make the choicest borders where they cannot be robbed by the roots of trees; see that the ground is good and rich, and that it is at least two and a half feet deep, so deep that, in a dry season, the roots can seek their supplies far below the surface. In planting, plant in naturally disposed groups, never repeating the same plant along the border at intervals, as is so often done with favourites. Do not always graduate the plants in height from the front to the back, as is generally done, but sometimes let a bold plant come to the edge; and, on the other hand, let ... a dwarf plant pass in here and there to the back, so as to give a varied, instead of a monotonous surface. Have no patience with bare gound, and *cover* the border with dwarf plants; do not put them along the front of the border only. Let hepaticas, saxifrages, Golden Money-wort, stonecrops, Forget-me-nots, dwarf phloxes, and many similar plants cover the ground among the tall plants — at the back as well as the front. Let the little ground plants form broad patches and colonies by themselves occasionally, and let them pass into and under other plants. A white lily will be all the better for having a colony of creeping Forget-me-nots over it in the winter, and the variety that may be thus obtained is infinite.

Thoroughly prepared at first, such a border might remain for years without any digging in the usual sense. When a plant is old and rather too thick, never hesitate to replant it on a wet day in the middle of August any more than in the middle of winter. Take it up, and put a fresh bold group in fresh ground; the young plants will have plenty of roots by the winter, and in the following spring will flower much stronger than if they had been transplanted in spring or in winter. Do not pay too much attention to labelling; if a plant is not worth knowing, it is not worth growing; let each good thing be so bold, and so well grown as to make its presence felt.

A friend and contemporary of William Robinson, Frank

Miles, was another early protagonist of the herbaceous border. He, too, stressed the importance of good soil preparation. Perhaps some of the treatment he suggests is almost too thorough for labour-starved gardens today, but his principles are wholly admirable.

Once the idea of 'a herbaceous border' is accepted (and Miles, unlike Robinson, actually uses the phrase), one thing, he says:

> is quite certain, we can never go back to the borders of one's ancestors in which every plant had a bare space of ground round it. In the spot where once a plant had bloomed, there was an end for the year of any flowers. Now a yard of ground should have bloom on it for at least eight months in the year, and this applies to every yard of ground in a really good mixed border. I am certain that, once a border is well made, it need not be dug up at all. But the question is – what is a well-made border? I think a border is not well made, or unsuitable for growing the most beautiful plants to perfection, unless it is as well made as a Vine border in a vinery. Why we should not take as much trouble with the garden border as the border of a conservatory I cannot imagine . . . The more I garden the deeper I get my drainage, and the fuller of sand and fibre my soil. I consider, first, that a border must have a bed of broken bricks or other drainage, with ashes over that, to prevent the drainage from filling up; secondly, that the bed of drainage must have 2 feet of light soil over it; thirdly, that that soil must have equal parts of sand, soil, and vegetable matter. A soil of these constituents and depths is never wet in winter and never dry in summer. During the dry weather I found soil prepared in this way . . . to be quite moist an inch below the surface, and I know in winter it always appears dry compared with the natural garden soil.

> But, for all practical intents and purposes, every 6 inches of ground could contain its plant, so that no 6 inches of bare ground need obtrude on the eye. Almost any kind of bare rock has a certain beauty, but I cannot say bare ground is ever beautiful. Well, supposing the back of the border filled with Delphiniums, Phloxes,

and Roses . . . and other summer and autumn-blooming plants, and supposing the border to be made as I have described it, I should carpet the ground at the back with spring-blooming flowers, so that when the roses are bare and the delphiniums and phloxes have not pushed above ground, the border should even then be a blaze of beauty. Crocuses, snowdrops, aconites, and primroses are quite enough for that purpose . . . And among the roses, and peonies and other medium-sized plants I would put all the taller lilies, such as require continual shade on their roots; . . . At the front of the border . . . I would have combinations, such as the great St Bruno's Lily and the delicate hybrid columbines . . . If once you get it into your head that no bit of ground ought ever to be seen without flowers or immediate prospect of flowers, heaps of combinations will immediately occur to those conversant with plants.

All this is excellently good advice, and interesting as an example of the new thinking in Victorian gardening, which must have been revolutionary. The idea of planting daffodils in a mixed border, except at the very back (as Frank Miles advocates) is not now considered to be practical: but in early spring, as can be seen from the pictures in this book, the Royal garden is full of bright colour from crocus and daffodil time until the herbaceous border is ready to come into its own, with a brilliance of tulips which fairly 'makes the rash gazer wipe his eye'.

Planted in a broad swathe, the whole length of the border, the tulips' very names seem to sound a fanfare – General Eisenhower (guardsman red), Gold Medal, Aristocrat (magenta), and Amethyst . . .

Victoria Sackville-West in her classic poem, 'The Garden', seems to exult in the names of tulips and in their colours.

> . . . earliest
> The Royal Princes of Orange and of Austria
> Their courtier the little Duc van Thol
> And, since the State must travel with the Church
> In plum-shot crimson, Couleur Cardinal . . .

and then

> Comes the tall Darwin with the waxing May
> Can stem so slender bear such sovereign head
> Nor stoop with weight of beauty? See, her pride
> Equals her beauty: never grew so straight
> A spire of faith, nor flew so bright a flag,
> Lacquered by brush-stroke of the painting sun.

Thus wrote that great gardener and poet. Never did green fingers wield so lyrical a pen.

The tulip season, thanks to thoughtful planting, lasts for many weeks, starting with the early singles, then the Triumphs, the Cottage tulips, the splendid Darwins and the last May flowerers. But it comes to an end finally, though by the time the last have faded and their petals lie in brilliant tatters on the ground, the herbaceous plants take over.

From then on the border grows in beauty every day, and among the many plants that compose it are Doronicum Spring Beauty which, with the tulips, is one of the earliest plants in the border to flower; *Lythrum salicaria*, the Purple Loosestrife; *Monarda didyma* (bergamot); the bronze form of Foeniculum, the dark-leaved, feathery herb, Fennel; the unusual purple thistle, *Cirsium rivulare*; the golden *Heliopsis patulum*; the scarlet *Lychnis chalcedonica*; Sidalcea Rose Queen; pink crinums and *Gypsophila paniculata* Bristol Fairy with its galaxy of flowers – and many more.

But one plant, at home equally in cottage gardens or in palace ones, is a particularly striking feature of the Buckingham Palace border in July, and must have special mention: delphiniums.

Though delphiniums have never played any part in literature, unlike the lily, the rose or the camellia, they are very special. Their very name is synonymous with blue; they are, unexpectedly, closely related to the buttercup, and a careful observer will notice that the leaves of the two plants are very much alike. Their name derives from *dolphin*, for Dioscorides, who wrote one of the earliest herbals, *De Materia Medica*, saw in a flight of fancy a remote resemblance between the delphinium's bud-form and a dolphin's head. Another name for delphiniums used to be the Flower of Ajax, though John

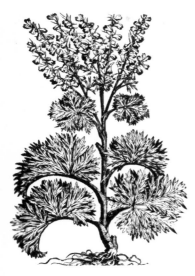

A Delphinium as illustrated in Gerard's *Herball*, published in 1597.

Gerard, whose famous book was published in 1597, refers to the flower ajacis as being of almost every colour except blue; and as being 'sometimes of a purplish colour, sometimes white, carnation and of sundry other colours . . . varying indefinitely according to the soil or countrye wherein they live.'

Old English names for the delphiniums or larkspur are Larkes Claws or Larkes Toes. Gerard advises its use, medically, for scorpion bite, and claims that it has a paralysing effect on all venomous insects.

Early in this century a special display of delphiniums at a flower show at Holland House caused a sensation, especially with 'some Japanese gentlemen . . . the delphinium being little known in their country'.

Yet there is little poetry about the delphiniums. They are beautiful . . . and blue: and in the book I wrote some years ago, *Flowers in History*, I once more quoted Victoria Sackville-West, and described her as coming down to earth with something of a bump when she described delphiniums as growing:'. . . in almost any kind of soil, light or heavy, and they will do their best for us, somehow or other, and they do respond to good treatment, and who does not? It is not a question of "feed the Brute, but feed the Beauty".'

Mr Nutbeam certainly knows how to feed the beauty, and to give delphiniums the treatment that they like. The delphiniums at Buckingham Palace make the glory of the herbaceous border in late June and early July, and are the admiration of the thousands of the guests at the Queen's garden parties. Some of the varieties that echo the colour of the summer sky, when the weather is kind, are Alice Artindale, Blue Celeste, Royalist, Stirling, Pyramus and Blackmore's Glorious.

XIX

The Rose Garden

Most of the roses grown in the garden of Buckingham Palace are to be found in the area of the Waterloo Vase and the Admiralty Temple Summer House.

Behind the Temple there is a large, half-moon-shaped bed of that excellent, vigorously growing rose Ann Cocker, with light vermilion flowers. This is grown both in bush form and as standards, an effective combination. As background to this bed is a curving pergola-screen, which throughout June and July is curtained with roses, among which are the vibrantly coloured Danse du Feu, the ponderously named, but beautifully blossomed, deep crimson Parkdirektor Riggers, and two other excellent German-raised roses, the creamy yellow Leverkusen and apricot-tinted Maigold. Here, too, Madame Gregoire Staechlin, surely one of the best of all climbing roses, shows its rich pink flowers in June but, sadly, in June only. It is a hybrid of two famous roses, Frau Karl Drushki and Château de Clos Vougeot. Two other roses which clothe the screen with flower in summer are the blood-red Altissimo, and the apricot-blushing Schoolgirl, the daughter of Coral Dawn and Belle Blonde, who has been brightening rose gardens since her first appearance in 1964.

In front of the Temple, and set in turf, are ten or more rectangular beds, each about eight yards by five in size. Here are grown, one variety to a bed, an impressive collection of both Floribundas and Hybrid Teas; among them Pink Parfait,

114

the name of which so aptly describes its pink petalled flowers, pale yellow at the base; City of Gloucester, a Hybrid Tea, with flowers of saffron and an upright habit of growth; Red Dandy, as debonair as its name implies, and resistant to wind and weather; the amber yellow Moonraker, a child on one side, of Pink Parfait; King Arthur, with gallant flowers of deep salmon and the crimson, English raised Stephan Langdon. Here, too, are two beds of that great new rose introduced last year and named after the Queen's Silver Jubilee, a Hybrid Tea rose which has been described as 'a confection of pink, peach and cream'.

Other roses in these luxuriantly planted beds, at their very best in June and July, are Alec's Red, with flowers the colour of ripe cherries; that old favourite, Sutters Gold, raised in America in 1950, and Madame Louis Laperrière, with flowers that are bright crimson, and heavily scented. The large square beds in which these roses are set have a background of tall ilexes with lower plantations of rhododendrons in front. Less formally situated, are groups of the so-called old-fashioned shrub roses which are so popular in every garden, whatever its size, today. 'So-called' because many are not really old; some of the best are hybrids introduced in the last half-century. To name just a few of such roses growing in the Royal garden, and laying their sweetness on the summer air, there is the still new, pink form of Nevada, covered with flowers every June; the much loved Blanc Double de Coubert, first introduced in 1892, with its white, scented, papery flowers, and golden autumn colouring and the imperial purple Hansa. There is also the yellow, strong-growing Frühlingsgold, considered by many to be the best rose ever produced by the brilliant German rose-grower Herr Kordes: it appeared in commerce as recently as 1937.

One last rose deserves special mention, Xanthina Canary Bird, with its coloured stems and butter-yellow flowers. This was the rose that that great connoisseur Miss Nancy Lindsay, who wrote so exuberantly of her favourite flowers, once described as having been 'first observed in a Cathayan garden about 1800', adding in triumphant vein: 'The tally of China's great golden roses is not yet told . . . gorgeous great shrubs with fee-fo-fum triangular thorns close set on cinnamon boughs and ferny leaves of jade-green hue. Their showers of

Rosa foetida bicolor

115

dog-roses are of a lovely golden lemon, and the orbicular hips glow like rubies.'

One of the great charms of 'old' roses lies in their names. Who could resist a rose which was the colour of 'Cuisse de Nymphe Emue' or the shape of 'Napoleon's hat'? 'Belle de Crécy' conjures up Proust's heartless heroine, and 'Hebe's Lip' promises flowers pink as Cupid's Bow. Many are called after kings and queens, cardinals and duchesses. But resounding as these rose names are, many others are called after quite ordinary-sounding women: Madame Hardy, for instance, or Miss Lowe, or Mrs John Laing. It would be interesting to know who they were. Betty Uprichard? Petite Lisette? Blanche Moreau? All we know of them is their names, evocations, perhaps of a sun bonnet glimpsed through rose-branches, a white frock, a pinafore, a parasol; nothing, really, but a faint scent of roses carried down the airs of time. As I once wrote many years ago: 'They were probably the obscure wives or daughters of dedicated rose-growers. Patient, long-suffering women who, as like as not, were dreadfully bored in life by their menfolk's passion. It is only fair that they should be rewarded with this kind of immortality.'

The Grey Border

One of the most attractive of all the plantings in the Royal garden is the Grey Border which was a present to Her Majesty the Queen – not to mark her Silver Jubilee, as might be thought, but some years before by Lord and Lady Astor of Hever as a Silver Wedding present.

A silver – or more prosaically – a grey garden, is no new idea. But grey plants must be grouped with thought and care. Gertrude Jekyll, one of the greatest of all gardeners once wrote:

> I am of opinion that the possession of a quantity of plants, however good the plants may be themselves and however ample their number, does not make a collection. Having got the plants, the great thing is to use them with careful selection and definite intention. Merely having them, or having them planted un-assorted in garden spaces . . . does not constitute a garden picture; and it seems to me that the duty we owe to our gardens and to our own bettering in our gardens, is so to use the plants that they shall form delightful pictures.
>
> It is just in the way it is done that lies the whole difference between commonplace gardening and gardening that may rightly claim to rank as a fine art. Given the same space of ground and the same material, they may either be fashioned . . . into a place of perfect rest and refreshment of mind and body . . . or they may be so misused that everything is jarring and displeas-ing.

It was the eminent Miss Jekyll who first had the brilliant idea of gardening in colours – of creating borders of predominantly one colour, sparked off by the inclusion in the planting of flowers or small shrubs of colours that are complementary. It is a sophisticated, and not easy, form of gardening, but one which, if carried out successfully, can be immensely effective and satisfying.

One of Miss Jekyll's most successful early essays in 'gardening by colours' was the creation of a grey border at her famous garden at Munstead Wood. Nearby was an orange border – a very different affair, and full of the most vibrant colour. The grey border was in delightful contrast. She describes it in her book, *Colour Schemes for the Flower Garden*.

'Perhaps the grey garden is seen at its best by reaching it through the orange borders.' Approaching the grey garden after the stronger colouring, Miss Jekyll found the effect 'surprising – quite astonishingly – luminous and refreshing . . . the grey and glaucous foliage looking strangely cool and clear'.

The grey border in the garden of Buckingham Palace makes much the same effect. It is ideally sited – for most grey and silver plants like full sun – on the south side of the high wall which divides the garden from the west end of Constitution Hill. Here a well-chosen collection of plants has been assembled. They are carefully planted, and each group of plants contrasts, either in leaf or flower or both with its neighbour as does, for instance, the feathery spikes of *Artemisia palmeri*, which, though a great spreader, is one of the most graceful of its family, with the lower cushiony growth of *Anaphalis triplinervis*.

Artemisia, for a plant with such a beautifully classical name, comes down to earth when addressed in the vernacular – its colloquial names being Mugwort, Wormwood, or Old Man – but by any name it is a first class plant. *Artemisia ludoviciana* is a degree less rampant than *A. palmeri*.

Another grey-leaved artemisia which I do not remember seeing growing in the grey border at Buckingham Palace but which might well find a place there, is *Artemisia arborescens*. This is a tall, shrubby plant which grows marvellously well in a much less exalted parterre – but one which is barely fifty yards from the Royal garden – in the mixed shrub border at Hyde Park Corner. *A. arborescens* was long thought to be half-hardy, but at Hyde Park Corner it has come through at least four London winters, and is now outgrowing its allotted space. It seems impervious to petrol fumes, lack of water in dry summers and downpours in winter. It is one of the most beautiful of all the 'silvers', and makes a handsome shrub between five and six feet in height.

The Palace border is planted with *Santolina incana* – the ever popular cotton lavender; the pungent leaves of this plant, in Tudor days, were used in cupboards as a deterrent to moths, hence its old-fashioned French name, guarde-robe. Thomas Tusser (1520–80) recommends this use for santolina in his work *A hundreth goode pointes of husbandrie*.

Lavender (*Lavandula spica*) has an important role to play in any grey border, especially Dutch Lavender, which has more lucent foliage than its English cousin. It is slightly smaller and more compact in growth and makes a better and more decorative hedge.

Another stand-by for any border of plants with grey or silver foliage is the simple *Stachys lanata*, colloquially and endearingly called either Lamb's Lug, or Jesus' Flannel. This has been grown in English gardens for centuries and must be one of the best loved of all plants. It seems indifferent to soil and will send up its quite handsome spikes of mauvish flowers with clockwork regularity in June. Some gardeners think that this spoils the effect of the plant, for stachys is almost always used as an edging. For these perfectionists a new strain has recently appeared on the market, and a very useful one, Silver Carpet. It never produces flower-spikes, and its silver velvet leaves are at their best in August and September when borders, however well-planned, are beginning to lose their early summer freshness.

A few more plants which add their individual tones to the grey border in the Royal garden must be mentioned: one is *Senecio laxifolius*, a plant from New Zealand which has won an important place in almost any scheme. Grey-leaved, and yellow daisy-flowered, it is one of the best all-round shrubs we have. Again, perfectionists quibble at its yellow flowers, but these, though too attractive to scrap when in their white twigged bud, can easily be snipped off before flowering. Teucrium, one feels, must be less hardy than it was when Gerard (1545–1612) wrote his famous herbal. For he recommends it, using its old name, germander, as making a good low hedge. It is a plant which is now treated as being only half-hardy, and does best if planted against a south-facing wall.

Ruta graveolens is another old-fashioned plant with bluish glaucous leaves which adds an unusual note of colour to any border. Canon Ellacombe in his *Plant lore and garden craft of Shakespeare* has a theory that: 'Rue was the English name for sorrow and remorse, and to rue was to be sorry for anything or to have pity . . Anything so bitter . . . must be connected with repentance. It was therefore the Herb of Repentance . . .' and in Shakespeare's *King Richard II*, rue was the gardener's 'Sour herb of grace'.

A new variety of *Ruta graveolens* has been in commerce for the last few years which has leaves of a more vivid blue than the type. It is called Jackman's Blue, and is a very beautiful plant indeed.

There are silver thymes in the grey border, and mints with leaves splashed with white, and grey-leaved sages. Like lavender and cotton lavender, these are all herbs, and almost all herby plants are worthy of a place in a border of grey and silver, for their leaves are often not only aromatic, but faintly furred with silver hairs. Herbs have a mystique and character of their own. Rudyard Kipling recognized this fact when he wrote:

> Excellent herbs had our fathers of old
> Excellent herbs to ease their pain
> Alexanders and Marigold
> Eyebright, Orris and Elecampane
> Basil, Rocket, Valerian, Rue
> (Almost singing themselves they run)
> Vervain, Dittany, Call-me-to-you
> Cowslip, Meliot, Rose of the Sun.
> Anything green that grew out of the mould
> Was an excellent herb to our fathers of old.

OPPOSITE
The north west corner of the Palace, overlooking the lawn – with roses in the foreground.

120

In July, in time for the Queen's garden parties, Delphiniums make a haze of blue in the herbaceous border. In the foreground white geraniums 'Princess Alexandra' have replaced the earlier tulips.

As the summer days pass, the border takes on warmer, more golden tones.

The Grey Border set with plants of different silver leaves was a silver wedding present to the Queen and Prince Philip in 1971. Among the plants in this very special border – just over the wall from Hyde Park Corner – are *Santolina incana, Anaphalis triplinervis* and the rarely grown *Teucrium fruticans.*

Geraniums being grown in quantity in the greenhouse area.

A flower arrangement made by Mr F. Kemp of the Royal Garden Staff for the Queen's tea table at a garden party.

XXI
The Cascade

The garden of Buckingham Palace is almost unique among Royal gardens in not having any statues, and it must also be one of the very few Royal gardens to be without a single fountain. It is difficult to imagine the garden at Versailles, or any Königliche Schloss, or even the garden of the Swedish country palace at Drôttningholm, in a climate far colder than ours, to be without statuary or ornamental *jets d'eau*. Neither is to be found in our own Royal garden. But there is a cascade, far smaller than the one at Blenheim, and less formal than the one at Chatsworth, which is still a charming and successful example of its kind.

Water in a garden is generally accepted as a blessing – and moving water especially so. The garden owner, even if his blessed plot is only the size of a small back yard, is accounted fortunate if he has water at his command. Victoria Sackville-West expressed her thoughts on water in four crystal lines:

> Water is living . . . springs from earth
> Whether from mountain poured in melting stream
> Or risen in the stones, a bubbling birth
> Struck by some Moses from a sombre dream.

OPPOSITE
Flamingoes (*Phoenicopterus ruber ruber*) in consultation on the lake (*see page 130*).

121

The cascade in the garden of Buckingham Palace can hardly be described as being poured from a mountain stream (its water is piped under the London streets) and its bubbling birth was conjured not by Moses, but by the command of the King of England. King George VI and Queen Elizabeth added much of interest to their London garden and the cascade was their idea, and a very happy one.

It lies on the west side of the garden, just over the wall from Grosvenor Place. In spring, it is in full beauty, with its rocky banks planted thickly with epimediums and other plants which enjoy a riparian life, all in a picturesque setting of young green foliage and the bright flowers of rhododendrons.

Garden Ornaments

(a) The Waterloo Vase, the Admiralty Temple Summer House and the Sundial

One side of the Waterloo Vase shows a seated Imperial figure, very like Napoleon, though the head has been roughly altered to look like the Prince Regent.

The Waterloo Vase stands in a glade of high trees – not far from the Admiralty Temple Summer House and the Rose Garden, and its history is an interesting one.

In 1805, soon after he crowned himself Emperor of the French, Napoleon set about finding European kingdoms, principalities and duchies for his numerous brothers and sisters. To Elisa Bacciochi, the plainest but one of the more able of his family, he gave the Principality of Lucca. Elisa was masterful, efficient, and intensely musical. She made Niccolò Paganini, the greatest violinist of the day, her musician-in-chief and also Commander of her Bodyguard. As he had recently become her lover, the second appointment was perhaps more appropriate than it appears at first.

Elisa set about governing her small territory with Napoleonic ability. Over the years, its has become customary to belittle and make fun of Napoleon's puppet rulers, but the impartial *Encyclopedia Britannica* describes Elisa's eight years' rule as bringing her domain 'marvellous prosperity'.

Among the many industries which she encouraged were the marble quarries at Carrara which had long been neglected and idle. With Elisa's encouragement, the quarries were soon producing marble by the ton and much of it was sculpted, some by the great Canova himself, into busts and statues of the Bonaparte family.

Napoleon was often bored by his sister who was continually badgering him with requests and reminding him how efficiently she was carrying out his instructions as to how to be a ruling Princess; but he was fond of her, as he was of all his family, and while inspecting a depot in Milan of marble from his sister's quarries, it is my personal theory that he sought to please her by commanding a huge vase to be cut from a single piece of marble. This in due course was fashioned, and shipped off to Paris. Around the sides of the vase were carved classical groups including one enthroned figure, which looked very like Napoleon himself, thinly disguised as a Roman Emperor.

In 1815, after Waterloo, such grandiose reminders of the Imperial past were an embarrassment to the restored Bourbons and the vase was offered by Louis XVIII to the Prince Regent, perhaps at the same time as he presented him with the Sèvres porcelain 'Table of the Commanders', now in the Blue Drawing Room at Buckingham Palace.

OPPOSITE
Her Majesty Queen Elizabeth the Queen Mother photographed before the war by Sir Cecil Beaton by the Waterloo Vase. The late King George VI and Queen Elizabeth, both knowledgeable gardeners, immensely improved the quality of the planting of the garden.

It is said that the face of Napoleon was, rather clumsily, altered to look like that of the Prince Regent. But we are also told, on the high authority of H. Clifford Smith, that the carvings on the vase are by Sir Richard Westmacott: on one side a battle scene, with cavalry in action, and on the other the George IV (or Napoleon) figure, with his attendants. Westmacott may well have altered the Emperor's face, but there must have been some carving there for him to have altered.

Whoever carved it, the Waterloo Vase stands fifteen feet high including the acanthus-carved base, and must be one of the largest single pieces of marble in the world.

William IV gave the vase to the National Gallery, opened in 1838, and there it stood until 1906, when the Trustees presented it to King Edward VII who had it placed in its present position. It features in one of the most attractive illustrations in this book: on page 125 a photograph taken by Cecil Beaton of Queen Elizabeth, the Queen Mother, and reproduced by Her Majesty's personal permission.

There is a story that, some years ago, when the vase was planted with pink ivy-leaved geraniums, a family of ducks found it a most desirable residence and nested there year after year. Now, however, the vase is left in its classical simplicity, unplanted, and the ducks have, no doubt, found alternative accommodation.

Within a stone's throw of the Waterloo Vase is the little eighteenth-century summer house which came early in this century from the garden of the Admiralty, when that building was enlarged and its garden built over. In design and feeling, the summer house recalls the work of William Kent who built the enchanting 'Green Seats' (Bowling Green Seats) which still stand in the garden at Rousham. The summer house in the Royal garden takes the form of an open temple – with four supporting pillars or herms in the shape of tritons.

As in thousands of gardens all over the country there is a sundial in the garden of Buckingham Palace. It is situated in full sun just as a sundial should be. Nearby, but not shading it, is a grove of trees planted by illustrious former occupants of the Palace, a copper beech planted by King Edward VII in

1902, a London plane by Princess Mary in 1913 and so on. There are elsewhere in the garden two sturdy oak trees grown from acorns which germinated in the years in which Prince Charles and Princess Anne were born.

Looking at the sundial, one is conscious of time: of time past, of time present and of the passing years. Queen Charlotte, first Royal occupant of Buckingham Palace, was hardly a great wit, but she could say pointful things. 'Time' she once described as 'so short to do anything in – so long to do nothing.'

The Admiralty Summer House has four supporting pillars or herms in the form of Tritons. It was moved to the Royal Garden from the garden of the Admiralty early this century.

Of all man-made ornaments for a garden, sundials seem the most suitable. Summer houses may be useful when it rains, and sundials go out of business. Temples may be more imposing. Statues have never enjoyed the popularity in English gardens that is theirs on the Continent and, even of metal or stone, they do not weather well in English winters. Garden seats are more usually serviceable than ornamental. A pity, for abroad they can be beautiful; and there are, or were, some supremely elegant garden seats in the Electoral garden at

Sundials 'symbolise time itself . . . time which sees the coming, and the going, both of cabbages and kings'.

Herrenhausen, in Hanover, home of the ancestors of our present reigning family.

But sundials seem an integral part of any garden. They symbolize time itself. Time which brings a garden to flower and fruit, and sees the coming, and the going, both of cabbages and Kings.

There is a beautiful French saying by De Fontenelle, comparing the life of a rose with the life of a man, and more especially with the life of a gardener. *De mémoire de rose, on n'a point vu mourir le jardinier*, which might be translated, 'As far as roses are concerned, the gardener never dies'.

Charles Lamb, the author and letter writer, was obsessed by sundials, and in one of his *Essays of Elia* he described the 'antique air' of the ancient sundials of the Inner Temple 'with their moral inscriptions, seeming coevals with that time which they measured', and he remembered how, as a child, he would 'watch the dark line steal imperceptibly on, eager to detect its movement, never catched, nice as an evanescent cloud, or the first arrests of sleep'. In comparison, he thought, 'what a dead thing is a clock, with its ponderous embowelments of lead and brass, its pert or solemn dullness of communication, compared with the simple, altar-like structure and silent heart language of the old sundial'.

For Charles Lamb, the sundial spoke of moderate labours, of pleasures not protracted after sunset, of temperance and good hours. It was the horologe of the first world. The shepherd 'carved it out quaintly in the sun' and turning philosopher by the very occupation, provided it with mottoes more touching than those on tombstones.

The sundial in the Royal garden bears no such telling inscription, no aphorism to point a moral and express, sometimes with some element of sanctimony, the feelings aroused by the thought of passing time. And yet inscriptions on sundials make rewarding study. Surely one of the best of all – optimistic and pointful – must be *Horas non numero sed serenas*, 'I only tell of sunny hours'. The best-known is *Tempus fugit*; the saddest, 'Time stays, we go'; the most cheerful, *A la bonne heure*. Most carping, 'Time wastes you, do not waste it', and downright sinister, a motto which I once found inscribed on an old sundial in a deserted garden in Scotland, 'It's later than you think'.

(b) The Flamingoes

The flamingoes, which are such a decorative and unexpected addition to the adornment of the Royal garden, first made their appearance there under twenty years ago. In any book on the story of the Royal garden which is divided approximately into different parts – History, The Garden Today and Garden Ornament, and Wild Life – it is a little difficult to decide where *Phoenicopterus ruber ruber* belong. Certainly not in the history section, as they are in no sense, though they may become so, in the same category as the ravens at the Tower, or the pelicans in St James's Park, which are part of the traditions of centuries. The flamingoes have only been in the Royal garden since 1961. They do not belong in the natural wild life section, because of all the bird life in the Palace garden the flamingoes are the least natural to their present habitat, having been artificially introduced, artificially fed and, in frosty weather, artificially housed (though this is less because they might suffer from cold than for fear that their legs might become frozen in the ice). In 'The Garden Today' they do find a place and I have finally decided to include them in the section devoted to 'Garden Ornament', for ornamental is what they first and foremost are, and they are there to be so – their 'simple doom', like Stephen Phillip's roses, being 'merely to be beautiful'. And flamingoes can look very like long-stalked pink roses. They are without doubt one of the most picturesque birds in the world.

Phoenicopterus ruber ruber, the twice-rosy flamingo, has two characteristics in common with all flamingoes which make it different from almost every other kind of bird. Its neck and legs are absurdly out of proportion with its body, and it turns its head upside down when it eats. This last curious fact is due to the function of a flamingo's top bill which acts as a kind of sieve. Through this the bird pumps muddy water and the foodstuffs it contains, and is aided in this operation by an abnormally large tongue and vestigial teeth.

A flamingo's diet consists of a natural soup made up of small aquatic animals, worms, plants and algae. Its tongue, being far larger in proportion to those of other aquatic fowls such as herons, makes it impossible for it to swallow large pieces of food like whole fishes. Flamingoes' tongues were themselves considered a culinary delicacy in Roman times.

130

Throughout history the flamingo has been hunted more for its magnificent plumage than for its edible qualities. But recently, as Oliver Austin tells us in his magnificent book, *Birds of the World*, the flamingo has had yet another enemy to contend with: the aeroplane. Unlike many wild creatures, the flamingo has never become accustomed to the aeroplane, and should 'a plane fly near a breeding colony the birds desert it in a frenzy, with disastrous loss of eggs and young'.

The greatest natural colonies of wild flamingo to be found in the world today are on the great lakes in Central Africa. I remember breakfasting on the shores of Lake Victoria, at Entebbe in Uganda with my war-time chief, Lord Wavell, before a meeting in Cape Town with Field Marshal Smuts. The lake was pink with flamingoes. Some were quite tame: tamer than the ones on the lake at Buckingham Palace, which resolutely refuse to pose for photographing. As some particularly friendly birds approached, Lord Wavell, never very conversational at breakfast time, nor at any other, for that matter, eyed them quizzingly and remarked: 'I would never have thought of using a flamingo as a croquet-mallet, would you, Peter?' A zany-seeming remark which, just too late, I realized was an allusion to *Alice in Wonderland*. How I wish I had been quick enough to reply: 'Nor a hedgehog for a ball.' But the moment had passed. *L'ésprit de l'escalier . . .*

The Buckingham Palace flamingoes are occasionally given a dietary treat and fed with packets of shrimps which are said to improve their colour. A distinguished entomologist tells how he was once standing near the Grosvenor Place gate of the garden, on the inside, talking to Mr Nutbeam. The gate bell rang and almost immediately a damp packet came flying over the wall and flopped at their feet – an express delivery of shrimps for the flamingoes from the local fishmongers.

Part III
Wild Life

XXIII

The Survey

In 1960, by gracious permission of the Queen, a survey of the wild life of the garden was begun. This followed two visits which David McClintock and two or three others had made to the garden to see the plants which grew wild or which had naturalized themselves there.

'Up to 1960,' writes David McClintock, 'very few other natural history records seem to have been made.' In 1926 three mosquitoes 'were noted breeding in rot-holes in trees'. In May 1929, Dr W. S. Bristowe, that most eminent of arachnologists (experts on spiders) spent some hours looking for specimens of his favourite creatures. (The author learned at this point that spiders are not insects at all, but Arachnids.)

In 1935, W. G. Teagle, inspecting the garden on behalf of the then Ministry of Works (now the Department of the Environment, under whose direction the Royal garden lies) saw a frog; and guests at Royal Garden Parties, between the cups of tea, had been known to spot one or two unexpected plants. 'This paucity' (of information), writes David McClintock, 'is in great contrast to the detailed records available in most groups from the neighbouring Royal Parks', and he goes on to say: 'The value of these botanical visits, and the observation then made of the remarkable quiet and shelter for wild life, argued well for a much wider investigation, permission for which was most generously granted.'

He made up his mind that the team chosen to carry out this investigation should be of important enough calibre to take the greatest advantage of the chance afforded them to examine such a unique terrain. Here, he realized, was an extensive area, a kind of veritable sanctuary, enclosed in the very centre of a great city; private and secluded for a century and a half, well stocked with trees, with thick plantations of shrubs, and extensive lake, comparatively free from human intrusion, and as yet unknown to students of wild life.

David McClintock co-opted the leaders of the privileged group, among whom were the spider-specialist Dr Bristowe, head of the Central Staff Department of I.C.I. and author of definitive works on his favourite Arachnids, *Comity of Spiders* (1939–40) and *The World of Spiders* (1958); the late Major Maxwell Knight, a great all-round naturalist and much-loved broadcaster, and Professor O. W. Richards of Imperial College, an expert on Diptera and Hymenoptera (two-winged flies, such as house flies, gnats etc., and four-winged insects, such as bees and wasps, respectively).

The team was subsequently further enlarged, with gracious permission, by the addition of specialists in various other fields, but the total party who would be actually carrying out their studies in the Palace grounds was kept as small as possible, so as not to cause disturbance. 'Specialists were needed,' David McClintock tells us, 'particularly for the smaller organisms, because non-specialists make very incomplete collectors, inexpert as to where to look, and what to expect to find.'

The sphere of activities was the garden and the terrace within the walls; the discoveries made by the team were of great interest, far greater than had been expected. The insect life was found to be extensive and far fuller than in neighbouring areas, such as St James's Park. 'In all,' wrote David McClintock, 'we identified over 2000 different taxa [sorts of plants and animals]. Well over 250 wild and naturalized plants have been listed, more than 50 not known elsewhere in Central London, and many others very rare there: two fungi proved to be new to the British Isles; the garden plants, important for birds and insects, were also listed.'

The movements and life-style of birds were carefully watched, and their nests mapped 'including a blackbird's on the ground by a path'.

Proportionally there were found to be many more birds in the Palace garden than in the neighbouring Parks.

The team discovered and identified several hundred moths. An oak planted by one of the Royal children was found to be suffering from scale insects and its unwelcome visitors were eliminated, whereupon the tree quickly started to put on new growth. The team's investigations also included a study of algae on and plankton in the lake.

The object of the operation was to 'fit the varying facets of the vast variety of life to be found into one whole: and to account . . . for apparent surprising rarities and scarcities'.

XXIV

Wild Plants

In any notes on the wild plants – as opposed to imported garden plants – in the garden at Buckingham Palace, it must be borne in mind that the whole area is a highly cultivated garden. It is not the same as a garden of thirty-nine acres would be likely to be in the country: partly cultivated, with lawns, borders, shrubberies, etc., but retaining on purpose, quite often, considerable wild areas for 'natural gardening', or doing so from necessity, owing to shortage of labour. The areas of the Royal garden which are left wild are a very small percentage of the whole, and no part lies more than a few yards from a 'gardened' part, or from an often-used path.

But an unexpectedly large number of plants have become naturalized, one of the more remarkable being the giant hogweed, a showy plant in any garden where there is room for it, and where it can be kept under control. Hogweed resembles cow parsley, with umbels of flowers, which can be eighteen inches across. Hence its American name of Cartwheel Flower. The one in the Royal garden, a smaller perennial, is much less common than the usual biennial: it has more pinnate leaves, and a less pungent odour when its stem is bruised (for some people, giant hogweed can produce a painful rash). The name of the plant in the Royal garden has defied investigation.

Another unusual plant in the garden is a chervil, *Chaerophyllum aureum* (*Chaero* from the Greek for pleasing, and *phyllon*, a leaf), a pretty herb with ferny aromatic leaves, which originates in Eastern Europe.

On the Mound are to be found three wild plants with good old English names – winter heliotrope (*Petasites fragrans*), golden garlic or moly (*Allium moly*) and dog's mercury (*Mercurialis perennis*). The last is seldom found growing wild in Central London; in ancient days, it was used to produce a blue dye, like woad. Winter heliotrope is one of the earliest of flowerers, and produces its sweetly-scented, dusty-purple heads of flowers in January.

There are tens of thousands of daffodils, crocus, aconites, scillas and snowdrops naturalized under the trees near the lake, and elsewhere in the garden, but these are what might be found, in smaller quantities, in any garden. Many of the bulbs, daffodils and narcissus in particular, were the gift of Queen Juliana of the Netherlands, whose mother Queen Wilhelmina spent much of the war in exile not far from the Palace in a house in Chester Square.

There are other interesting plants which have made themselves quite at home round the lake. *Senecio doria* has settled down to a riparian existence by the waterside, and two plants, which have certainly been introduced, *Cyperus longus*, or galingale, a rush-like plant with erect chestnut-coloured inflorescenses and *Gunnera manicata*, the largest of the well-known and pictorial 'giant rhubarbs' (of which it is no relation) which is a native of Brazil as already noted.

In a well-kept garden such as the Queen's, brambles are swiftly dealt with, but the so-called American cut-leaf bramble *Rubus laciniatus* whose home country David McClintock tells us is unknown, is allowed garden space, though kept within bounds.

The weeds in the garden are so few, and so intrepid, that on account of their boldness and British persistence, some deserve a mention, and mention in English too: Two Gallant Soldiers, Shepherd's Purse, Redleg, Lesser Wartcress, Ivy-Leaved Speedwell, Sticky Groundsel, Nipplewort, Sharp-leaved Fluellen. The list is much longer, but for all that, weeds in the garden are few and far between.

One casualty must be noted. Until 1961, when Hyde Park Corner was enlarged and a small slice of the Royal garden north-west of the wall was cut off, there was a pleasing plantation to be seen from Grosvenor Place which I remember well. It included the towering cartwheel heads of the Giant Hogweed, already mentioned; a beautiful specimen of the Willow-leaved Pear, *Pyrus salicifolia*, one of the best small trees with silver foliage, and 'Buckingham Palace's special hawkweed, *Hieracium lepidulum* var *haematophyllum* which is now no more'.

In conclusion to this section on the wild and naturalized

plants in the Royal garden, one can not do better than to quote David McClintock's concluding paragraph to his chapter on the subject.

One of the handsomer weeds left growing by the lake is an uncommon form of perennial Hogweed (*Heracleum*).

> Some 475 species of plants have been recorded in recent years from Central London in an area of some 12,500 acres. The mere fact that well over half of these (excluding planted narcissus, etc.) have been seen wild in the 39 acres of the Palace garden, many of them unrecorded or very scarce elsewhere in Central London, speaks for itself.

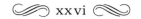

Birds

Taking into consideration the smaller acreage of the Royal garden as compared with the far greater size of the other open spaces round about, a proportionately greater variety of birds nest in the garden at Buckingham Palace than anywhere else in London. The following table* for the years 1961–62 shows clearly how the figures compare:

Buckingham Palace Garden   39 acres 20–21 breeding species

St James's and Green Park   105 acres 16–17 breeding species

A duck's nest and eggs at the base of the wall separating the Royal Garden from Hyde Park Corner.

*By courtesy of the British Ent. Nat. Hist. Soc.

Waterfowl observed recently on the lake in Buckingham Palace garden – woodcuts by Thomas Bewick (1753–1828).

Little Grebe or Dabchick (*Podiceps ruficollis*) found its last Inner London refuge on the Palace lake.

Pochard (*Aythya ferina*).

Tufted Duck (*Aythya fuligula*).

Gadwall (*Anas strepera*).

| Regents Park and Primrose Hill | 574 acres 26–28 breeding species |
| Hyde Park and Kensington Gardens | 635 acres 22–23 breeding species |

Thus it can easily be seen that 'there is a general tendency for the variety of nesting species to increase with area in the Parks, but the Garden, the smallest of the four areas, had a greater number of breeding species than St James's Park and Green Park together, and only a little below that of the very much larger Hyde Park and Kensington Gardens'.

Some of the birds which have nested regularly in the Royal garden are the great tit, blue tit, wren, mistle thrush, song thrush, blackbird, robin, spotted flycatcher, dunnock and pied wagtail. Chaffinches and jays, for some reason, were not noted as nesting there.

The lake, with its thick vegetation, now left uncut until after the nesting season, offers welcome hospitality to several kinds of duck, such as mallard, tufted duck and pochard. One pair made themselves so much at home as to eschew the cover offered by the waterside and nested, in the open, at the base of the wall of the garden near Hyde Park Corner – within a few feet of the busiest traffic junction in London. A photograph of this nest, taken by Dr J. D. Bradley, is shown on page 140.

Summing-up:

> The garden shows a good variety of breeding birds compared with the Royal Parks, especially in view of their size. There are, however, no species not found nesting elsewhere in Inner London, although up to some ten years or so ago, the dabchick (*Podiceps ruficollis*) found its last Inner London refuge there, a pair apparently breeding in most years on the lake. It is not known whether its disappearance is due to the removal of suitable nesting cover, or changes in food supply in the lake.

Fish and Amphibians

There are very few species of mammals to be found in the Royal garden, and this pattern follows that set by the other Royal Parks of Central London. The presence of the house mouse (*Mus musculus*) and the brown rat (*Rattus norvegicus*) has been recorded.

In 1963, Mr David McClintock, in an interview reported in the *Sunday Times*, appealed for help when he wrote:

> As for bats – they have been sighted in St James's and Hyde Park. But though we have been in for hours at dusk, and asked the gardeners and policemen to keep watch we still haven't a record of a single bat in Buckingham Palace gardens. So if anyone on guard, or at a garden party, or anything, has ever seen a bat at the Palace, will they please tell me?

Since then, an occasional bat, *Pipistrellus pipistrellus*, has been seen, but not many.

Fish are not plentiful in the lake, though Mr Nutbeam reports that in the very severe winter of 1962–3 some, including quite large ones, were frozen in the ice. Gudgeon (*Gobio gobio*) have been caught by net. And dace, roach and perch, some fairly sizeable, have been taken. One perch, caught in 1970, was fourteen inches long.

The attempt to establish rainbow trout in the lake in 1902 has already been recorded (see page 89).

There are few frogs and toads in the garden, though when the Cascade was made in 1960–1, Mr Nutbeam remembers an ancient toad (*Bufo bufo*) being found under a large rock. This dearth of frogs and toads is almost certainly due to the fact that the lake, owing to cultivation around it and an increasing number of resident water fowl, has become unsuitable for them. 'Toads', Major Maxwell Knight tells us, 'are notoriously

selective in their spawning ponds, and conditions must be just right for them to breed year after year. It is well established that toads will desert a pond for no obvious reason – not enough is yet known about the chemical content of the favoured waters, nor the exact type of aquatic plant life necessary for the development of tadpoles.'

As much has been made so far of the unexpected forms of wild life and the rarities to be found in the Royal garden, the solitary toad found there might come under the heading of rarity; toads and toad life, at this juncture, deserve a mention.

Toads are some of the most fascinating of creatures, and the most harmless. But for centuries they have had a bad name. The exiled Duke in *As You Like It* thought of the toad as 'ugly and venomous'; in the old days, toads were supposed to suck milk from cows, rob birds' nests, have the evil eye, and their saliva (which they do not possess) was said to be poisonous to dogs. To be caught with a pet toad meant death under suspicion of witchcraft and the free-thinker, Lucilio Vanini, was burned at the stake for such an offence in 1619. The French naturalist, Comte de Lacépède who lived in the last century and should have known better, was quite unbalanced in his hatred of toads:

> Public opinion has long stigmatized this disgusting beast, whose proximity revolts us. Everything about it . . . and its very name is vile. It is the fortuitous product of dust and moisture . . . the angry glitter in its eye is revolting – its colour, dingy, its breath foul: it opens hideous jaws when it is attacked. It would seem that Nature has only created the toad to emphasise the beauty and nobility of her other creatures.

Poor toad. The most faithful, intelligent, harmless and fastidious of animals.

And Kenneth Grahame's picture of the conceited, boastful 'Mr Toad' is quite a wrong one. There is no creature more docile. If toads drove cars, they would never be caught speeding.

Years ago Jean Rostand, son of the more famous Edmond and a student of wild life, wrote a fascinating book about toads,

Luperina testacea Schiff.
Flounced Rustic

Euplexia lucipara L.
Small Angle-shades

Phlogophora meticulosa L.
Large Angle-shades

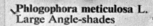

Thalpophila matura Hufn.
(*cytherea* F.)
Straw Underwing

Petilampa minima Haw.
(*arcuosa* Haw.)
Small Dotted Buff

Caradrina morpheus Hufn.
Mottled Rustic

Celaena leucostigma Hübn.
(*fibrosa* Hübn.)
Brown Crescent

Hydraecia oculea L.
(*nictitans* Borkh.)
Common Ear

Cucullia absinthii L.
Pale Wormwood Shark

Mormo maura L.
Old-lady

Arenostola pygmina Haw.
(*fulva* Hübn.)
Small Wainscot

Coenobia rufa Haw.
(*despecta* Treits.)
Rufous Wainscot

<u>**Lygephila pastinum**</u> Treits.
Blackneck

Plusia chrysitis L.
Common Burnished Brass

Plusia pulchrina Haw.
Beautiful Golden Y

Plusia gamma L.
Common Silver Y

Unca triplasia L.
Dark Spectacle

Unca tripartita Hufn.
(*urticae* Hübn.)
Light Spectacle

<u>**Scoliopteryx libatrix**</u> L.
Herald

very different from his father's classic work (the very opposite of a treatise on wild life) about the captive L'Aiglon. I read Jean Rostand's book forty years ago, and I have never forgotten it. Here are some true facts about toads.

Toads are vertebrates, and have hands with five fingers. Though most people think of them as a sort of reptile, they are more nearly related to man than they are to fishes.

There are said to be no toads in Ireland, Corsica or Majorca.

Toads have beautiful golden eyes and three eyelids. The third lid is transparent, like a contact lens. They can only close one eye at a time. Their long pink tongues are attached at the front of their mouth, rather than at the back.

They go pale all over when frightened.

The story that toads can be hermetically sealed up in a wall or under a stone for years is not quite true. As they breathe, they need air – but very, very little. An experiment carried out one-hundred-and-fifty years ago proved that toads enclosed in chalk or plaster containers (which are porous) and buried three feet in the earth, were still alive after thirteen months. Those enclosed in stone containers, and sealed up, were dead. A toad in an earthenware jar, sealed up, once survived for six years. Though they are voracious feeders, they can fast for years.

Toads can be frozen absolutely solid, so that their eyes are 'like hailstones', and survive.

Toads do not drink through the mouth, but through their skin.

OPPOSITE
Twenty-three moths caught in the Royal Garden (*see chapter XXVII*). The central one in the bottom row is a native of Tropical Africa and may have been introduced in the clothing or luggage of a visiting Commonwealth prime minister.

The common toad (*Bufo bufo*).

They can survive decapitation for several hours.

They are not, as generally supposed, sensationally long-lived – though some have lived for forty years, and become 'colossal'.

Toads are strictly carnivorous. They live on worms, beetles, caterpillars and ants; they eat bees and do not feel their stings. They never eat any kind of plant.

Toads have no teeth, practically no neck; when feeding they crush their victims against the roof of their mouth.

Toads are good gardeners, as they eat almost all wingless insects. Their friends say that they only eat harmful insects, but this is not true. Though there happen to be rather few useful insects, they do eat almost all of them (except slugs and snails).

The female toad is dumb – the male can make sounds. Jean Rostand says that a male toad sings when he makes love.

A toad's love life is interesting. After six months' hibernation a toad mates, always at about the same time in March. Its stomach is empty, but it does not think of food, only of love; it makes for the nearest water, sometimes travelling miles to get there, and travelling always by night. Once in water, it waits. At the end of March, the female appears, driven by the same instinct, exactly a fortnight later. Perhaps she is drawn by the attraction of water, or by the male's seductive voice; for several nights before she comes, he utters a small inviting croak.

As soon as they meet, the male toad gets on top of the female, and enfolds her in a tight embrace. Sometimes, in his ardour, he strangles her. With his front legs (or arms) fully occupied, his long hind legs hang loose, ready to kick away any other rival suitor. This coupling lasts for several days. Finally the female lays her string of eggs 'like crystal tubes, studded with black pearls'; the male fertilizes them, 'singing' according to Rostand, as he does so. Love-making over, the toads separate, and become land creatures once more. They start to eat, to prepare for the next hibernation, but male and female have lost interest in each other, and they go their own ways.

Is the toad poisonous? They have long been thought to be so; to a certain extent they are, but they are practically harmless to humans.

In the unlikely event of a human being injecting himself

with the sweat of a toad, some slight irritation might ensue. Dogs and cats would suffer more. Grass snakes consume large quantities of toads, with no ill effects. So have humans, and their flesh has even been considered delicate.

So much for toads.

During the time that the survey was being made in the Royal garden, to everyone's surprise, what were referred to as two red-breasted frogs were found. Mr Nutbeam reports them as having breasts red as a robin's – 'not quite as dark, but a real red breast'. No red-breasted frog is known in England, according to the Natural History Museum; so what were found may have been two fire-bellied toads. This species has been found in Britain, but very rarely, and never for long. Its Latin name is *Bombina bombina*.

There are only three frogs wild in Britain, the common frog, *Rana temporaria*, the edible frog, the rare *Rana esculenta*, and the marsh frog, *Rana ridibunda*. How the red-breasted toads (or frogs) got into the garden is a mystery, and they have not been seen since their initial discovery.

Lepidoptera

Zeuzera pyrina, the Leopard Moth, and larva.

The garden at Buckingham Palace offers promising conditions for the lepidopterist. It is full of well-grown trees of many different kinds. These all offer sources of food for a wide range of lepidoptera. Most of the large trees and plantations of shrubs are to be found on the outer edges of the garden (originally planted for privacy, and following Pope's precept 'to conceal the bounds') leaving a central space for the great lawn and the lake. This last is well stocked with duck, and is the haunt of the famous flamingoes. 'The presence' of these different water-fowl, the entomologist Dr J. D. Bradley of the Commonwealth Institute of Entomology and the late Mr R. M. Mere tell us, 'is of indirect benefit to the lepidoptera, since during the breeding season, extensive areas of vegetation bordering the lake are left undisturbed and allowed to grow wild'. These areas of natural growth, of reeds, ferns and different knotweed – especially *Polygonum cuspidatum* – make the ideal breeding ground and living space for insects.

To help the studies of the survey team, permission was given to set up a mercury vapour light trap for moths.

The trap used to catch moths and other night-flying insects.

This light trap method [the experts say] has the great advantage that, once switched on at dusk, it operates without more attention until dawn, when the lamp is put out and the trap covered until the catch can be examined at leisure. It has, however, certain draw-backs, chief of which are the very definite limitations as regards efficiency. The immense 'attractive' power to night-flying insects in general, and lepidoptera in particular, of ultra-violet light emitted by the mercury vapour lamp can be largely nullified by adverse climatic or physical conditions such as strong wind, or counter-attractions such as street lamps. Further, the flight habits of certain species of moths are such that, although the moths fly readily to the light, they seldom if ever enter the trap, but rest on the nearby ground. To overcome this weakness, we visited the trap in the early evening whenever possible. These occasions were few and far between and a number of 'untrappable' species have undoubtedly escaped notice. The trap has, nevertheless, been invaluable in the present survey, and has furnished an impressive number of records and valuable data on the frequency of occurrence of many species.

Polygonum cuspidatum flourishes by the lake where clumps are left uncut. Its stems and side branches provide food for the rare *Monochroa hornigi*, shown on page 151.

Five-spot Burnet (*Zygaena trifolii*) one of the less frequent visitors to the garden.

Orgyia antiqua and larva.

Zygaena filipendulae The Vapourer Moth, and larva. The female is wingless.

The sustained and continuous operation of the trap during the period of survey, was 'entirely due to the enthusiastic collaboration of Mr F. C. Nutbeam'. The report continues:

Mr Nutbeam undertook the onerous task of operating the trap on prearranged nights, or nights he thought favourable for moths, and one or two of us would visit the garden the following day and examine the catch. On occasions when neither of us could go, Mr Nutbeam examined the catch himself. He would box alive anything that looked unfamiliar, releasing the rest. In this way a number of records were obtained which would otherwise have been missed, and we acknowledge with pleasure the contribution made by Mr Nutbeam to this survey. He spread his enthusiasm to some of his staff, and they brought for identification a number of moths and caterpillars found in the garden . . .

And it was Mr Nutbeam who, in June 1962, caught in the daytime the only specimen of *Zygaena trifolii* (Five Spot Burnet) found in the garden.

The general reader would be daunted by the detailed examination and description of all the lepidoptera found in the garden, mostly moths with a wing-span of less than an inch, many named only in Latin and familiar only to an expert.

Some of the more unexpected discoveries made (by Dr Bradley and Mr Mere) include: *Lampra fimbriata* (broad bordered yellow underwing), an essentially woodland species; *Tinea columbariella*, a clothes moth of which the larva is to be found in pigeons' nests; *Cucullia absinthii* (wormwood shark); *Ostrinia nubilalis* (European corn borer) and *Caradrina ambigua* (Vine's rustic). These last two moths feed on artemisia (mugwort) of which, when the survey was being made, there was very little in the garden. Garden forms of artemisia (*A. palmeri* and *ludoviciana*) were planted recently in some quantity in the new Grey Border, so the number of Ostrinia and Caradrina may increase.

Other unexpected finds were some moths of which the larva feed on conifers; fifteen years ago there were few conifers in the garden, and indeed conifers at that time were not supposed to thrive under city conditions. Recently more have been

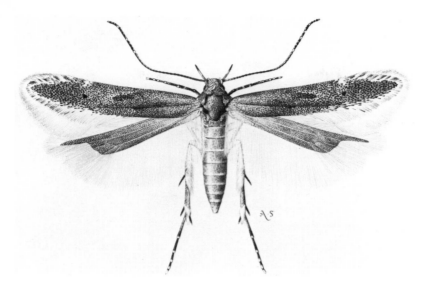

A specimen of very special interest was caught in the light trap, *Monochroa hornigi*, the first one ever to be caught in the British Isles. Lifesize its wingspan is half an inch. A drawing by Arthur Smith (Dr. J. D. Bradley).

planted, and thanks to the cleaner air of Central London, these have prospered.

A specimen of a small moth of very special interest was caught in the light trap, *Monochroa hornigi*, the first one ever to have been caught in the British Isles. This species occurs (Dr Bradley writes) in Austria and Germany, and its larva is known to feed in the stems of polygonum, several species of which were growing by the lake, and elsewhere in the garden. A detailed drawing in the possession of Dr Bradley of this beautiful creature is to be found above. Several more specimens of this moth have since been taken in the Royal garden, the most recent in June 1976.

Having mentioned several unexpected finds in the Royal garden, a few surprising absentees or rarities might now be noted. The borders and shrubberies being largely free of weeds, thanks to the labours of Mr Nutbeam and his team, there are practically no nettles. That is doubtless the reason for the scarcity of three widespread and common species of moth,

Sphinx ligustri, the Privet Hawkmoth.

Hypena proboscidalis (snout moth), *Eurrhypara hortulata* (small magpie moth) and *Pleurotypa ruralis*, whose favourite food is the nettle. The absence of these three species was noted in the survey report, but they have since been taken on several occasions by Dr Bradley.

Some other notable absentees were certain species, of the family Geometridae, moths 'which rest by day on tree trunks, walls etc., and rely on cryptic colour and marking for protection'. The absence of these may be due to the very large bird population of the garden. Birds as well as moths find the quiet, seclusion and rich planting of the garden a sanctuary, and one form of wild life does not necessarily respect another. In short, the birds have eaten the insects. One can not have it both ways.

Butterflies are not numerous, and very few species have been noted. The colour picture facing page 144 includes almost every species of butterfly that has ever been seen: all the specimens in the group were actually netted in the Royal garden.

The survey mentioned above covered a period of only three years, from 1960 to 1963, but permission to continue running the light trap was granted and it has been run annually from spring to autumn by Dr Bradley and Mr Nutbeam up to the present time. Observations on the lepidoptera in the garden thus cover a remarkable span of seventeen years, and the total number of species of butterflies and moths recorded to date is nearly five-hundred, amounting to more than one-fifth of all the species found in the British Isles.

The continuous monitoring of an insect fauna can provide interesting and valuable ecological data, and reflects subtle changes and fluctuations which take place and which might otherwise escape notice. For instance, it would appear that because of the cleaner air which London now enjoys, 'suburban' and 'rural' species of lepidoptera are beginning to move into the metropolis and some have taken up residence in the Royal garden. One such 'indicator' of atmospheric improvement is the tiny gold and purple azalea moth, *Caloptilia azaleella*, which first appeared in the garden about five years ago and according to Dr Bradley is now quite common, its larvae mining the leaves of the azaleas.

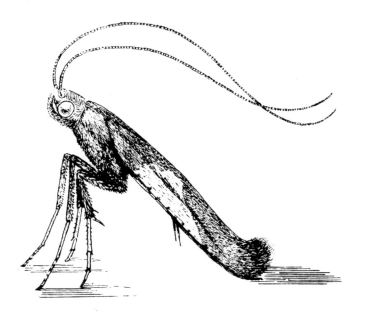

Caloptilia azaleella, the gold and purple Azalea Moth, which lives on the leaves of Azaleas and, since the air of London has become cleaner, has moved into the Royal Garden. It is shown in its resting posture. Life-size its wingspan is half an inch. F. C. Fraser, DEL.

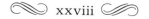

xxviii

Spiders and Insects

This chapter is not called spiders and *other* insects. As has been noted earlier in this section, spiders (Arachnids) are not classed scientifically as insects.

In the invaluable book from which so much has already been quoted, the chapter entitled 'Land Invertebrates other than Insects' by D. S. Bristowe, contains a letter quoted from Sir Clive Wigram (afterwards Lord Wigram) expressing King George V's 'delight' that a survey of the spiders in the Royal garden had yielded such a successful catch. This catch, made one May morning in 1929, had amounted to twenty-six species.

The garden was not considered then to be extraordinarily rich in Arachnids, possibly due to the acidity and the heavy soot deposits on the leaves and branches of trees and shrubs. The much fuller survey, made thirty years later, yielded a richer bag – though no real rarities were found; the one discovery which occasioned any surpise was that of *Dictyna viridissima*, 'a small (4mm) green spider which spins an inconspicuous flat web over a hawthorn or hazel leaf on trees growing close to the lake'.

One interesting spider which disappeared from the garden, between 1929 and 1960, was the little *Segestria florentina*. This was once common in the old masonry of Westminster Abbey and the buildings of the area, and had been found by Dr Bristowe in the crevices of the walls of the Royal garden. It is a spider which is a native of southern Europe, and 'has a tubular body, an inch long when fully grown and well fed. It lives in a silk tube in crevices, from which it darts to catch any insect which touches one of the long straight threads radiating outwards from its entrance'. But, since the brickwork of the wall of the Royal garden has been repointed, Segestria has disappeared.

A visit to the cellars of the Palace yielded the daddy-long-legs spider, *Pholcus phalangioides*, and a smaller relation with a

Araneus diadematus

154

blue body, *Physocyclus simoni*. The latter is often imported in the straw of cases of French wine.

It is outside the scope of this book to describe the snails and slugs, earthworms, stoneflies, bird-lice, sucking lice and fleas found or not found in the garden. But it would seem 'that about 10 per cent of the British insect fauna might be expected to occur in the garden'.

For specialists, the following figures might be of interest. They show the number of species collected in the Royal garden out of the total number of British species, in five groups:

Oonops pulchev

Collembola (spring tails)	36/260
Heteroptera (insects whose wings are coriaceous at the base and membraneous at the tip, e.g. plant bugs, etc.)	32/509
Aphidoidea (greenfly)	58/370
Trichoptera (caddis-flies)	13/188
Agromizaedae (leaf miners)	16/224
Total of all together	155/1551.

This would seem to point out 'the abundance of tree-living insects and the shortage of species living in the herbage layer. This is mainly a characteristic of a well-kept garden in which the lower, accessible layers are regularly trimmed, and in which weeds and insect pests are discouraged . . .'

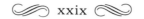 xxix

Postscript

This, then, is the story of the garden of Buckingham Palace, its history, how it is today, and a description of some of the unusual specimens of wild life which make their home in it.

The garden is the Queen's garden, just as the Palace is her London home. The point has already been made that though the Palace garden is not open to the public, as the Queen's Gallery is, it is a garden which thousands of people visit every year; more than visit most of the private gardens in the country which are regularly open for charity. For months on end, it is true, the garden at Buckingham Palace is an area of quietness in the middle of a great city: it is beautifully kept, by a surprisingly small staff, as befits the garden of the Queen of a nation of gardeners. Though for some time every summer the garden is very far from quiet, as preparations have to be made for the reception of the thousands of guests at the garden parties and other functions. But for long periods it is the Queen's private garden, and nothing more. It is hers to use as thousands of other women use their gardens: to relax in, to take the dogs out in, to walk out in, and to look for the first snowdrops, to see if the daffodils are showing colour, or if there are buds on the rhododendrons.

The Queen is one of the hardest worked women in the world. Her professional existence began when she was a child and will continue, unremittingly, for the rest of her life. She is not only the one woman in the world who has known and had close dealings with every Prime Minister of this country for the last twenty-five years, but who has also met, on equal terms, almost every head of state since 1952. Since she has been Queen there have been seven Presidents of the United States, and five Presidents of France. During her reign there will be more.

It is good for us to know that, after a long day with the Red Boxes, with her secretaries, with her ministers, advising and being advised, suggesting, restraining, encouraging or deciding, the Queen is able sometimes, not to forget the continuing cares of her unique office, but to put them aside for half an hour by walking round her garden, listening to the birds and smelling the scent of mown grass.

Perhaps for a few moments, for her time must always be short, she may dead-head some roses, pull out some weeds, and forget who she is. Though the hum of traffic can always be heard beyond the bird-song, let us hope that these moments do happen, when the Queen can be alone in her garden, in the very heart of London, in the very heart of her country.

Index

Folios in *italic* indicate illustrations; *f.* indicates facing page

Abbot, Rev Charles, 47
Abraxus grossulariata (magpie moth), *152*
Acer palmatum Atropurpureum, 94
  A. palmatum Senkaki (coral bark maple),
    94
  A. saccharinum (silver maple), 94
Achillea (yarrow), 87
aconites, 111, 138
Admiralty Temple Summer House, 124,
  126; *f.97, 127*
Aesculus indica (Indian chestnut), 84; *f.48,
  f.49*
Aglais urticae (small tortoiseshell), *f.144*
Agromizaedae (leaf miners), 135
Ailanthus altissima (Tree of Heaven), 94–5
Aiton, William Townsend, 47, 51, 52–3, 56,
  58, 93
Albert, Prince, 56, 58, 62, 66, 68, 70, 89;
  61, 62
Alexandra, Queen, 74, 96–7
Allium moly (golden garlic, moly), 137
Anaphalis triplinervis, 118
Anas strepera (gadwall), *141*
Andromeda dealbata, see *Zenobia
  pulverulenta*
  A. polifolia (bog rosemary, moonwort),
    104–5
Anne, Queen, 30–2, 51; *32*
Anthemis nobilis (camomile), 85; *85*
  A. nobilis Treneague, 85
Aphidoidea (greenfly), 155
Arctia caja (tiger moth), *f.16, f.144*
Argemone lacianta, 20
Arlington, Earl of (Henry Bennet), 22, 24,
  25–9
Arlington House, 26, 28, 32
Artemisia arborescens, 118–19
  A. ludoviciana, 118, 150
  A. palmeri, 118, 150
Arundo donax, 87
Aston, Lord, 18, 21
Aucuba japonica (spotted laurel), 92
Augusta, Princess, 50–1
Austin, Oliver, 131
Aythya ferina (pochard), *141*
Aythya fuligula (tufted duck), *141*
Azalea mollis, *101*
Azalea moth (*Caloptilia azaleella*), *153*

Bacciochi, Elisa, 124
Banks, Sir Joseph, 47, 48
Bats, 143
Bean, W. J., 91, 94, 103
Beech (*Fagus sylvatica*), 92
Bennet, Henry, 22; *see also* Arlington, Earl
  of
Bennet, Lady Isabella (Duchess of Grafton),
  28–9, 30
Bent grasses, 84
Bergamot (*Monarda didyma*), 112
Betula pendula (silver birch), 92
Bird of Paradise flower (*Strelitzia reginae*),
  47; *f.17*
Blackbird, 135, 142

Blackfield, J. M., 81
Blore, Edward, 59, 78
Blue tits, 142
Bog rosemary (*Andromeda polifolia*), 104–5
Bombina bombina (red-breasted frog), 147
Bombyx mori (silkworms), 17; *f.16*
Bowden, Jean, 48
Bradley, Dr J. D., 142, 148, 150–3
Brambles, 138
Brimstone (*Gonepteryx rhamni*), *f.144*
Bristowe, Dr W. S., 90, 134–5, 154
Broad bordered yellow underwing (*Lampra
  fimbriata*), 150
Brown, Lancelot (Capability), 52
Brown, Mr (gardener), 81
Brown rat (*Rattus norvegicus*), 143
Buckingham, Catherine, Duchess of
  ('Princess Buckingham'), 37, 38–41, 95
Buckingham, Edmund 2nd Duke of, 38
Buckingham, John 1st Duke of (John
  Sheffield, Earl of Mulgrave), 32–3, 36–7,
  42, 58; *31*
Buckingham, House, 32–3, 36–7, 38–41, 42,
  50–1; *34–5, 40, 41*
Buckingham Palace, 51 ff.
Budding, Edwin, 83
Buddleia alternifolia (butterfly bush), 95
  B. davidii, 95
Buff-tip (*Phalera bucephala*), *f.144*
Bufo bufo (toad), 143–7
Bulrush (*Scirpus lacustris*), 87, 89–90
Butterflies, 152
Butterfly bush (*Buddleia alternifolia*), 95

Caddis-flies (Trichoptera), 155
Caloptila azaleella (azalea moth), 153; *153*
Camden, William, 19–20, 85
Camellias, 99–102
  Adolphe Audusson, 101
  Alba Simplex, 101
  Althiiflora, 101
  Countess Lavinia Maggi, 101
  Donation, 101
  Gloire de Nantes, 101
  Lady Vansittart, 101
  Princess Bacciochi, 101
  C. saluensis, 101
  C. sasanqua, 101; *99*
  Tricolor, 101
Caradrina ambigua (Vine's rustic), 150
Caryopteris clandonensis, 106
Cascade, 56, 121–2, 143
Cassiopes, 105
Castanea sativa (sweet chestnut), 96; *f.33*
Celastrina argiolus (holly blue), *f.144*
Ceratostigma willmottianum (smoke tree),
  106–7
Chaerophyllum aureum (chervil), 137
Chaffinches, 142
Chamaemelum nobilis, 20, 85
Chamomile, 20, 85
Charles I, 18, 28
Charles II, 25, 30–2
Charlotte, Princess (daughter of George IV), 59

Charlotte, Queen (Princess Charlotte of
  Mecklenberg-Strelitz), 42–3, 47–50, 83,
  127; *43, 50*
Cherries, flowering, 100
Chervil (*Chaerophyllum aureum*), 137
Cinnabar (*Tyria jacobaeae*), *f.144*
Cirsium rivulare, 112
Coade, Eleanor, 80
Cole, Mr (gardener), 81
Collembola (spring tails), 155
Columbines, 111
Common reedmace (*Typha latifolia*), 87
Copper beech, 126
Coral bark maple (*Acer palmatum* Senkaki),
  94
Cornus sibirica, 94
Cotinus coggygria, 106
Cotton lavendar (*Santolina incana*), 119–20
Courroux, Mr (gardener), 81–2
Cowell, Sir John, 63
Crinums, 112
Croggan of Lambeth, 81
Cromwell, Oliver, 19, 22
Crocuses, 111, 138; *f.48*
Crow Fields, 32, 51
Cucullia absinthii (wormwood shark), 150
Cynthia cardui (painted lady), *f.144*
Cyperus longus (galingale), 138

Dabchick (*Podiceps ruficollis*), 142; *141*
Dace, 143
Daddy-long-legs spider (*Pholcus
  phalangioides*), 154
Daffodils, 111, 138; *f.49*
Deilephila elpenor (elephant hawk), *f.144*
Delphiniums, 110–11, 112–13
  Alice Artindale, 113
  Blackmore's Glorious, 113
  Blue Celeste, 113
  Pyramus, 113
  Royalist, 113
  Stirling, 113
Denbigh, Earl of, 89–90
Devonshire, Duke of, 29, 30
Dickens, Charles, 44–5
Dictyna viridissima (spider), 86, 154
Dog's mercury (*Mercurialis perennis*), 137
Dog's tail grass, 84
Doronicum Spring Beauty, 112
Dryden, John, 24, 26, 28
Ducks, 90, 148
Dunnock, 142

Eastlake, Sir Charles, 67
Edward VII, 71, 89–90
Edwards, Sydenham, 67
Elephant hawk (*Deilephila elpenor*), *f.144*
Elizabeth II, H.M., 74–5, 95, 134, 156–7
Elizabeth the Queen Mother, H.M., 95, 100;
  125
Ellacombe, Canon, 120
Epimediums, 122
Etherege, George, 24

Etty, William, 67
European corn borer (*Ostrinia nubilalis*), 150
Eurrhypara hortulata (small magpie moth), 152
Evelyn, John, 19, 22, 26

Fagus sylvatica (beech), 92
Fennel (Foeniculum), 112
Field, Michael, 101
Fish, 89, 143–4
Five-spot burnet (*Zygaena trifolii*), 150
Flamingoes (*Phoenicopterus ruber ruber*), 130–1, 148; *f.121*
Forget-me-nots, 109
Frogs, 132, 147
  common (*Rana temporaria*), 147
  edible (*Rana esculenta*), 147
  marsh (*Rana ridibunda*), 147
  red-breasted (*Bombina bombina*), 147

Gadwall (*Anas strepera*), 141
Galingale (*Cyperus longus*), 138
Garden parties, 9, 70–5, 84, 86
Garden Pavilion, 56, 62, 65–9; *f.32, 65, 68*
Garden tiger (*Arctica caja*), *f.144*
George II, 38
George III, 41, 42–4, 46, 48–9; *43*
George IV, 50–1, 53, 56–7, 58–9, 64, 74, 78, 93, 95, 103, 125–6
George V, 71, 78, 154
George VI, 75, 81, 95, 100
Gerard, John, 112–13, 119
Gibson, Edmond, 19
Gobio gobio (gudgeon), 143
Golden garlic (*Allium moly*), 137
Golden moneywort, 109
Golden privet, 92
Gonepteryx rhamni (brimstone), *f.144*
Goring House, 21–4, 26; *26*
Goring, Lord (Earl of Norwich), 21–2
Graeme, Bruce, 15, 18, 30
Grafton, Duke of, 28–9
Grasses, 84–5
Great tit, 142
Greenfly (Aphidoidea), 155
Grey Border, 117–20
Grey, Lord, 59
Grüner, Ludwig, 66–7
Gudgeon (*Gobio gobio*), 143
Gypsophila paniculata Bristol Fairy, 112

Hawkweed (*Hieracium lepidulum* var *haematophyllum*), 138
Hedley, Olwen, 47–8
Heliapsis patulum, 112
Henry VIII, 19
Hepaticas, 109
Herbert, Charles, *see* Sheffield, Charles
Heteroptera, 155
Hieracium lepidulum var *haematophyllum* (hawkweed), 138
Hogweed, 137, 138; *139*
Hollies (ilex), 92
Holly blue (*Celastrina argiolus*), *f.144*
House mouse (*Mus musculus*), 143
Humphrey, Mr (gardener), 81
Hypena proboscidalis (snout moth), 152

Ilex (holly), 92, 115
Inachis io (peacock butterfly), *f.144*

Indian chestnuts (*Aesculus indica*), 84; *f.48, f.49*
Ivy, 75
Ivy-leaved speedwell, 138

James I, 14–18, 93, 97–8
James II, 38, 95
Jamison, Mrs, 66–7
Japanese knotweed (*Polygonum cuspidatum*), 87, 148; *149*
Japanese tree peony Mrs William Kelway, *104*
Jays, 142
Jekyll, Gertrude, 87, 117–18
Jesus' Flannel (*Stachys lanata*), 119
Jordan, Dorothy, 58–9

Kamel, Georg, 99
Kent, William, 52, 126
Knight, Major Maxwell, 135, 143
Knollys, Lord, 89

Lake, 53, 56, 58, 84, 87–90, 143; *f.129*
Lamb's Lug (*Stachys lanata*), 119
Lampra fimbriata (broad bordered yellow underwing), 150
Landseer, Edwin, 67
Large white (*Pieris brassicae*), *f.144*
Larkspur, *see* Delphiniums
Lavandula spica (Lavender), 119, 120
Lawn, 20, 74, 82, 84–5
Leaf miners (Agromizaedae), 155
Leopold of the Belgians, King, 61, 68, 100
Leslie, Charles, 67
Lesser knotweed (*Polygonum compactum*), 87
Lesser wartcress, 138
Leucothoës, 105
Lightfoot, John, 48
Lindsay, Nancy, 115
Linnaeus, 94, 99, 102
Liriodendron tulipifera (tulip tree), 95
Little grebe (*Podiceps ruficollis*), *141*
London plane (*Platanus acerifolia*), 91–2, 127
Longford, Elizabeth, 70
Loudon, John, 93
Louis XVIII, 124
Lower Crow, 22
Lychnis chalcedonica, 112
Lythrum salicaria (purple loosestrife), 112

Mackenzie, Compton, 58
Maclise, Daniel, 67
Magnol, Pierre, 102
Magnolias, 100, 102–4
  M. grandiflora, 103
  M. kobus, 102
  M. liliflora nigra, 104
  M. sieboldii (syn. *parviflora*), 102
  M. soulangeana, 103–4; *f.65*
  M. soulangeana Picture, 104; *f.65*
  M. stellata, 102–3
Magpie moth (*Abraxus grossulariata*), 152
Magpie moth, small (*Eurrhypara hortulata*), 152
Mallard, 142
Mary, Queen, 69, 71, 74–5
McClintock, David, 10, 134–5, 138–9, 143
Melbourne, Lord, 59
Mercurialis perennis (dog's mercury), 137

Mere, R. M., 148, 150
Michaelmas daisies, 106
Michaux, André, 93
Miles, Frank, 109–10, 111
Milton, John, 66
Mint, 120
Mistle thrush, 142
Moly (*Allium moly*), 137
Monarda didyma (bergamot), 112
Monochroa hornigi, 151; *151*
Moonwort (*Andromeda polifolia*), 104–5
Morus alba (white mulberry), 17–18, 98
  M. nigra (black mulberry), 17, 98
Moths, 135
Mound, 53, 56
Mulberry Gardens, 14–18, 19, 21–4, 30; *26*
Mulberry trees, 17–18, 97–8
Mulgrave, Earl of (John Sheffield, Duke of Buckingham), 30–2
Mus musculus (house mouse), 143
Muscus palustris, 20

Napoleon, 124, 126
Nash, John, 56, 58, 78–9, 81; *53*
Natural History of the Garden of Buckingham Palace (survey), 10, 134–55
Nipplewort, 138
Norwich, Earl of, *see* Goring, Lord
Nutbeam, Fred, 10, 81–2, 85, 98, 99, 108, 113, 131, 143, 147, 150–2; *100*
Nyroca ferina (pochard), 86
Nyssa sylvatica (Tupelo), 95

Orgyia antiqua (moth), *130*
Osborne, Mr (gardener), 81
Osmunda regalis (Royal fern), 20, 87; *88, f.129*
Ostrinia nubilalis (European corn borer), 150
Ox-eye daisies (*Telekia speciosa*), 87

Painted Lady (*Cynthia cardui*), *f.144*
Palmerston, Lord, 89
Pararge aegeria (speckled wood), *f.144*
Parkinson, John, 93
Paulovna, Anna, 95
Paulownia tomentosa (*imperialis*), 95
Peacock butterfly (*Inachis io*), *f.144*
Peonies, 108, 111
Perch, 143
Petasites fragrans (winter heliotrope), 137–8
Phalera bucephala (buff-tip), *f.144*
Pheasants, golden and silver, 61
Phloxes, 109, 110–11
Phoenicopterus ruber ruber (flamingos), 130–1; *f.121*
Pholcus phalangioides (daddy-long-legs spider), 154
Phormium tenax, 88
Photina beauvardiana, 95
Phragmatobia rubiginosa (ruby tiger), *f.144*
Phragmites communis, 87
Physocyclus simoni (spider), 155
Pied wagtail, 142
Pieris, 105–6
  P. forrestii, 105; *f.80*
Pieris brassicae (large white butterfly), *f.144*
  P. rapae (small white butterfly), *f.144*
Pipistrellus pipistrellus (bat), 143
Platanus acerifolia (London plane), 91, 127
Pleurotypa ruralis (moth), 152

Plumbago, 106
Pochard, 86, 142; *141*
Podiceps ruficollis (dabchick, little grebe), 142; *141*
Polygonus compactum (lesser knotweed), 87, 151
P. *cuspidatum* (Japanese knotweed), 87, 148; *149*
Pope, Alexander, 52–3
Primroses, 111
Privet hawk-moth (*Sphinx ligustri*), *f.144, 151*
Pye, Henry James, 47
Pyrus salicifolia (willow-leaved pear), 138

Queen flower (*Strelitzia reginae*), 47; *f.17*
Queen's House, 42–6, 49–50

Rainbow trout, 89–90, 143–4
Rana esculenta (edible frog), 147
    R. *ridibunda* (marsh frog), 147
    R. *temporaria* (common frog), 147
Rattus norvegicus (brown rat), 143
Ray, John, 99
Red Admiral (*Vanessa atalanta*), *f.144*
Redleg, 138
Rhododendrons, 115, 122
Rhus cotinus, see *Cotinus coggygria*
Richards, Prof O. W., 135
Richardson, Prof Sir Albert, 78
Roach, 143
Robin, 142
Robinson, William, 108–10
Roses, 111, 114–16
    Alec's Red, 115
    Altissimo, 114
    Ann Cocker, 114
    Belle Blonde, 114
    Betty Uprichard, 116
    Blanc Double de Coubert, 115
    Blanche Moreau, 116
    Château de Clos Vougeot, 114
    City of Gloucester, 115
    Coral Dawn, 114
    Danse du Feu, 114
    Elizabeth of Glamis, *f.75*
    Frau Karl Drushki, 114
    Frühlingsgold, 115
    Hansa, 115
    Herr Kordes, 115
    King Arthur, 115
    Leverkusen, 114
    Madame Gregoire Staechlin, 114
    Madame Hardy, 116
    Madame Louise Laperrière, 115
    Maigold, 114
    Miss Lowe, 116
    Moonraker, 115
    Mrs John Laing, 116
    Nevada, 115
    Parkdirektor Riggers, 114
    Petite Lisette, 116
    Pink Parfait, 114–15
    Red Dandy, 115
    Schoolgirl, 114
    Silver Jubilee, 115

Stephen Langdon, 115
    Sutter's Gold, 115
    Xanthina Canary Bird, 115
Rostand, Edmond, 144–5
Rostand, Jean, 144–6
Royal fern (*Osmunda regalis*), 20, 87; *88, f.129*
Rubus laciniatus (American cut-leaf bramble), 138
Ruby tiger (*Phragmatobia rubiginosa*), *f.144*
Ruta graveolens, 120
    Jackman's Blue, 120
Rye grass, 84

Sackville-West, Victoria, 111–12, 113, 121
Sages, 120
Sagittaria, 87
St James's Park, 19, 21, 32, 90, 135, 140
Santolina incana (cotton lavender), 119
Saxifrages, 109
Scale insects, 135
Scillas, 138
Scirpus lacustris (bulrush), 87
Sedley, Catherine, 38
Sedley, Sir Charles, 23, 38
Segestria florentina (spider), 154
Senecio doria, 138
    S. *laxifolius*, 119
Seymour, Robert, 33
Sharp-leaved fluellen, 138
Sheffield, Charles (C. Herbert), 41
Sheffield, John, *see* Buckingham, Duke of; and Mulgrave, Earl of
Sheffield, Major Reginald, 41
Shepherd's Purse, 138
Sidalcea Rose Queen, 112
Silver birch (*Betula pendula*), 92
Silver maple (*Acer saccharinum*), 94
Sitwell, Sir Osbert, 75
Small tortoiseshell (*Aglais urticae*), *f.144*
Small white (*Pieris rapae*), *f.144*
Smith, H. Clifford, 22, 51, 78, 126
Smoke tree (*Cotinus coggygria*), 106–7
Smooth-stalked meadow grass, 84
Snout moth (*Hypena proboscidalis*), *152*
Snowdrops, 111, 138
Song thrush, 142
Sophora japonica, 94
Soulange-Bodin, Etienne, 103
Speckled wood (*Pararge aegeria*), *f.144*
Sphinx ligustri (privet hawk-moth), *f.144, 151*
Spotted laurel (*Aucuba japonica*), 92
Spotted flycatcher, 142
Spring tails (Collembola), 155
Stachys lanata (Jesus' Flannel, Lamb's Lug), 119
    Silver Carpet, 119
Stallenge, Jasper, 18
Stallenge, William, 16–18
Steegman, John, 66–7
Sticky Groundsel, 138
Stirling, Mr (gardener), 81
Stonecrops, 109
Strelitzia reginae (Bird of Paradise flower, Queen flower), 47; *f.17*

Sundials, 128–9; *128*
Swamp cypress (*Taxodium distichum*), 93–4
Swans, 90
Sweet chestnut (*Castanea sativa*), 96; *f.33, 96*
Sydney, Lord, 63

Taxodium distichum (swamp cypress), 93–4, 106
Taylor, Geoffrey, 83
Teagle, W. G., 134
Telekia speciosa (Ox-eye daisies), 87
Teucrium, 119
Thomas, Mr, 63–4
Thornton, Robert, 48
Thymes, 120
Tinea columbariella (moth), 150
Toads (*Bufo bufo*), 143–7; *145*
Trichoptera (caddis-flies), 155
Tree of Heaven (*Ailanthus alitissima*), 94–5
Tufted ducks (*Aythya fuligula*), 142; *141*
Tulips, 108, 111–12; *f.81*
    Amethyst, 111
    Aristocrat, 111
    General Eisenhower, 111
    Gold Medal, 111
Tulip tree (*Liriodendron tulipifera*), 95
Tupelo (*Nyssa sylvatica*), 95
Turner, E. S., 71
Tusser, Thomas, 119
Two Gallant Soldiers, 138
Tyria jacobaeae (cinnabar), *f.144*

Upper Crow, 22

Vanessa atalanta (red admiral), *f.144*
Vapourer moth (*Zygaena filipendulae*), *150*
Viburnum carlesii, 107
Victoria, Queen, 56, 59–60, 61–4, 66–7, 70–1, 99–100; *61, 62, 70*
Vine's rustic (*Caradrina ambigua*), 150

Walpole, Horace, 38, 40, 42, 52
Waterloo Vase, 124–6; *123, 125*
Webb, Sir Aston, 78
Weeds, 138
Westmacott, Sir Richard, 126
William III, 32, 95
William IV, 58–9, 64, 126
Willmott, Ellen, 106
Willow-leaved pear (*Pyrus salicifolia*), 138
Winter heliotrope (*Petasites fragrans*), 137–8
Wise, Henry, 30, 51
Wormwood shark (*Cucullia absinthii*), 150
Wren, 142
Wycherly, William, 24
Wyness, Mr (gardener), 81

Yarrow (Achillea), 87

Zenobias, 105
    Z. *pulverulenta*, 106
Ziegler, Philip, 59
Zygaena filipendulae (vapourer moth), *150*
    Z. *trifolii* (five-spot burnet), 150; *150*